In My Mother's Footsteps

An Odyssey of Faith and Courage

A Memoir
Rebecca Barber

trimarkpress

The copyright for this historical non-fiction memoir, which reflects real events pertaining to Jewish refugees fleeing the Nazis in the years during World War II, remains with its author(s). The publisher and editors gratefully acknowledge the individuals who granted us permission to publish their original work.

Published by TriMark Press, Inc., Deerfield Beach, Florida.

LIBRARY OF CONGRESS CATALOGING-IN-PUBLICATION DATA

In My Mother's Footsteps

Rebecca Barber

P. CM.

ISBN: 978-1-943401-56-7

LIBRARY OF CONGRESS CONTROL NUMBER: 2019936922

D-19

10 9 8 7 6 5 4 3 2 1

First Edition

Printed and Bound in the United States of America

A publication of TriMark Press, Inc.
368 South Military Trail
Deerfield Beach, FL 33442
800.889.0693
www.TriMarkPress.com

In Loving Memory

of my Mother,
Leah Steppel z"l *
For trusting the puzzle would be solved.

* z"l refers to Zichrona Livracha, "May her memory be a blessing."

iii

Dedication

This book is dedicated to my husband,
Sandy Barber, for encouraging me to dream.

Foreword

$\mathcal{M}$ost of the story of
my mother, Leah Steppel, is
illuminated by her diary. Since her
diary was first printed in 1996, new
and enlightening information on
her life and her journey has burst
forth with the help of Dr. Olivia
Mattis and the Sousa Mendes
Foundation. I am forever grateful.

So much has transpired since
the book's first printing. Sadly, my
brother, Mark, met his untimely
passing at the age of 48. It was a telling testimony that Mark's
friends and Jewish community in Seattle were with him every
step of the way.

"You reap what you sow," our Mother always said. Mark's
supportive, loving "chevrah" is evidence to the time and
energy Mark placed on being part of a Jewish community. He
brought dignity to the Dykan name with his courage and faith
through the last days of his life.

May his memory be
for a blessing.
R.D.B. 7/18

V

In other areas, life has moved forward.

My children have grown and have children of their own. My husband, Sandy, and I have retired and moved to South Florida which has proven to be the best time of our lives. I have picked up where I left off years ago: speaking at high schools and communities in Palm Beach County about my mother's diary and its importance in this day and age.

The Barber Boys, 2018
From left: Elliot, Jonah, Mitchell, Jake and Sandy Barber

About Dr. Monroe Helfgott

*I*t was my lucky day when I read in our community's newsletter that a new resident was going to start a memoir writing club. Not a bad idea, I thought, having just returned with Sandy from an extraordinary experience in Europe.

I thought it would be a good idea to put our journey in writing. Unfortunately, I had no idea how to begin. All the events and reactions I experienced were jumbled up in my mind, causing a paralyzing affect.

Then along came Monroe, better known as Monty, my soon-to-be mentor and friend. He is a published author whose desire to help others was evident from the start. On the road to complete this memoir, Monty provided me the guidelines to follow through his lesson plans, exercises and mantra: Just Write.

Monty's steadfast faith in me and this project certainly played a role in its completion. His ability to make order of the time spans, seemingly disconnected pieces of a puzzle, and to guide me to sort out my thoughts was invaluable. Thank you, Monty.

And many thanks ...

Writing a book is harder than I thought and more rewarding than I could have ever imagined. Having an idea and turning it into a book is as hard as it sounds. I thank my "sisters" and "brothers" in Valencia Pointe who have been a source of encouragement all along this journey.

I would also like to thank and acknowledge my editor and TriMark Press Publishing Director Lorie Greenspan. I had very specific and sometimes impossible design requests. Lorie remained steadfast and patient throughout the process. All of her efforts helped to make this book complete; I could not have done it without you, Lorie.

Amann's Nähseide seit 80 Jahren bewährt

4 Km. / Heerlen / Holland
13 " / Antwerpen / Belgium
Refugade über
Lapurne, überen "
Pas de Calais / France
1 Tg. (Neew Chapel, / "
2 Tg. (Lceun) / "
1 Tg. Bethune / "
½ Tg. St. Paul / "
¼ Tg. Abberville / "
1 Tg. Tréport / "
3 Tg. Paris / "
4 Wch. Bordeaux / "
1 Tg. Hendaye / "
2 Tg. Bayonne / "
1 Tg. Irün / Espaniole
1 Ncht Salamanka / "
1 " Villar Formosso / Portugal
1 " Pampilhosa / "
Curia / "

Many have wondered how I knew what route Leah and the Steppels traveled between 1939 and 1941 to escape the Nazis. It was my good fortune that Mother left this detailed running list of every city, town, and village she (and the family) passed through.

$\mathcal{M}$y momentous journey to truly walk in my mother's footsteps was organized by the Sousa Mendes Foundation, named in honor of Aristides de Sousa Mendes, Consul General of Portugal, stationed in Bordeaux, France, circa June 1938-40.

In direct defiance of President António de Oliveira Salazar, dictator of Portugal, Sousa Mendes risked his life, family, career and fortune issuing visas and passports to over 30,000 refugees, a significant number of them Jews. Everything Sousa Mendes held dear was destroyed when he disregarded President Salazar's orders to reject refugees attempting to escape through Portugal.

Based on the diary my mother kept during her journey of escape, as well as research conducted by The Sousa Mendes Foundation, we obtained conclusive evidence that both my mother and all members of her immediate family had been

Our group followed this route with the Sousa Mendes Foundation from Saturday, June 25, to Tuesday, July 5, 2017.

issued visas by Sousa Mendes in Bordeaux, signed by the consul secretary Manuel de Vieira Braga, with official powers of his office.

My trip, or as I prefer to describe it, a journey or an odyssey, which my husband and I participated in from June to July, 2017, took us along the Bordeaux to Lisbon portion of the Steppels' flight. Accompanying us were twenty-eight fellow journeyers, who are direct descendants of visa recipients.

The Sousa Mendes Foundation today works tirelessly to popularize his name, bestowing admiration he so truly deserves. In 1966, the State of Israel posthumously honored him with the title, "Righteous Among the Nations."

Table of Contents

PART 1
The Memoir

PART 2
The Diary
Translated and edited
First Publication,1996

PART 3
Portions of the Diary in its original German

PART 4
Documents, Visas, & Artifacts

Prologue

*B*lood streams down across the man's face from head wounds inflicted by kicking jackboots and punching fists carried out by five brown shirt Nazi goons. Caught, the Düsseldorf synagogue sexton, Moses Steppel, attempted to save a sacred Torah scroll. Stumbling out through synagogue doors, he staggers over cobblestone streets running half blind, blood trickling from head wound blows from assaulting fists of hate. His only thought – get home. Making his way up several flights of stairs, he reaches the family apartment, hammering at the door. Horrified at his blood-spattered sight, the family is numb struck. The beating, a warning, a sobering message: flee Nazi Germany.

The eldest daughter wipes blood with a towel then turns toward her mother, her sister and brother. Her clear blue eyes speak with certainty and determination. Their only course of action – run for their lives as soon as possible. Several weeks later, the family prepares but is still in Düsseldorf and the message is repeated. A message written in blood soaked shattered glass window fragments of Jewish businesses, homes and synagogues.

The eldest Steppel family daughter is raised in Düsseldorf, Germany, until the Night of Broken Glass, when there was looting, humiliating, beating, and killing Jews in an orgy of violence. Her youthful, clear azure blue eyes are deeply saddened, yet resolute. The family, now outcast fugitives, are led with strength and cunning by nineteen-year-old Leah Steppel, my mother. They run, they hide for nearly two years, always one step ahead of relentless Nazi pursuers, hell-bent with a single purpose – Jewish capture and extermination.

Polish passport that saved the Steppel family
from immediate expulsion from Germany.

ב"ה

18 January, 1939

Lena Steppel

"*A*pproximately four weeks later, in November, (Crystal Night 9/10), the real excitement began. The October episode had just been a prelude. A young Jewish boy, 17 years of age, shot and killed a German legate in Paris. Following this occurrence all the synagogues in German cities were set on fire in the middle of the night; all Jewish stores were plundered and smashed; show windows were nailed up with boards. It was the greatest scandal that people ever lived to see. With 20 to 25 men they broke into private residences of the Jews, demolished and destroyed everything breakable. Even the people were not spared.

I myself saw on that day a girl with a totally disfigured face, completely battered and swollen. All the German citizenship were led away and put into concentration or labor camps.

The Poles saved themselves in consulates. We also went there too. Since there was only one room at our disposal, it got pretty filled up, because people came from all the towns and surroundings. There was no place left to sit down. We were standing all the time; even the hallways were full of people."

"*T*hen the greatest calamity began: all Polish Jews had to leave Germany! In the evening, at exactly 12 o'clock midnight in October of 1938, there was a knock on our door, the police were standing outside and demanded entrance. They ordered my parents to immediately pack all their valuables and come with them. With this they coldly declared that my parents would never again see their residence. My parents did not believe the officials, and went along, as they were, with empty hands. My brother was, at the time, in Frankfurt at the Yeshiva. I, myself, was not home, but in the hospital. Only my little sister was at home, and she had to go along (with my parents).

At the police station they met many more Jews of the city. They had all come with bag and baggage. In short: all Jews were transported in cattle cars to Poland, except those who did not have their Polish passports."

Kasernenstraße 20 Synagogue, one block from
the Steppel apartment, before Kristallnacht.

Modern day Memorial in Düsseldorf for the destroyed synagogue.

Above: Wallerstrasse 10, the Steppel residence, in 1938, Düsseldorf. It is the third building from the right, upper four windows. One can see the beautiful synagogue in the upper left corner. *Below:* Synagogue set on fire and looted during Kristallnacht.

June 4, 2017

Carefully reviewing our journey's itinerary, I realize that specific locations along the preplanned Western European route are, in fact, a close duplication of the road my mother, her parents and siblings journeyed along to escape encroaching Nazi armies. Days before we are to fly to Europe, The Foundation informs us that a large percentage of refugees were, in fact, Jewish, and able to, through Mendes's help, prevent capture, deportation, and eventual extinction.

It's within this historical truth we begin upon a momentous, personal journey. And it is my hope and desire to unravel numerous questions embedded within my mother's diary pages. Such uncertainties include the unexplained diary gaps during my mother's two-year escape. As to this one specific mystery, I can only assume these gaps occurred because the family's priority must have been to travel in great haste from one location to another. I truly hope to illuminate unexplained pieces of my mother's past.

Checking calendar dates, our departure quickly approaches. And in my heart and mind, I embrace all that is to be discovered.

June 15, 2017

A shutter of apprehension washes over me. Methodically, I move in slow motion compiling travel documents, clothing and other necessities as I prepare to walk in the footsteps of my mother, who was barely nineteen years old when she led her family ever onward during the years 1939 to 1941.

More than seven decades have passed and today, June, 2017,

I enter within the modernity of the Miami Airport, focused and resolute through a tunneled boarding ramp ushering me within the belly of a Paris-bound jetliner. Fellow passengers find their way to assigned seats while others struggle, shoving carry-on luggage deep into overhead compartments.

Travelers, youthful and elderly, talk amongst themselves. I cannot hear their voices, for within this slow motion moment, voices fall mute upon my ears. Engines roar, thrusting the streamlined jet above the tarmac runway. I ignore the noise. Buckled in, I glance at my cabin window, squeezing my husband's hand. He alone reconnects me to the here and now. Yet, I feel another force pulling at me, leading me into the past.

Straining to retain focus within the moment, I try to read. My fingertips glide across words artistically scribed upon well-worn pages, my mother's secretive diary. The words blur, however, and I tire. The precious diary slips from my fingers. Again my window, inches away, beckons. I stare blankly as the plane moves forward, bringing my past into view. Letting go, I slip dreamily into decades and places that were a part of my mother's life, and are soon to be a part of my own.

And I think, it all began with a phone call ....

The Steppel family in 1935, from left: Itta, Otylia Lea, Henni, Pincus (Paul), Mojzesz (Moses)

PART 1
THE MEMOIR

Düsseldorf, Germany
Revelations

*H*ow is it possible that the untimely death of a four-year-old child could wipe away any hesitation the Steppel family may have harbored to remain in Germany after Hitler's rise to power and growing Jewish onslaught?

August 8, 2012

Walking in the door on August 5, 2012, I do not immediately check the voice mail for my landline. But by 8:30 that evening, I find a moment to listen to a blinking message. I am taken aback by the accent of the caller, but then recognize the voice as German, speaking in perfect English.

"My name is Hildegard Jakobs, and I am calling from Düsseldorf, Germany. I want to know if I can speak with Rebecca Dykan Barber, daughter of Leah Steppel. I am Deputy Director of the Düsseldorf Memorial Center. If I have the correct person, please contact me. My e-mail and phone number are left on this recording."

Hildegard Jakobs continues. "I have in my possession the diary of Leah Steppel. A friend of yours brought it to us over ten years ago." Ten years! I am startled by her words. A friend? Who could that be? I absolutely cannot recall anyone we knew having traveled to Düsseldorf, Germany. Perhaps a member of my large Israeli family on my father's side. Many of them love to travel, and do. I wanted so to call her, but calculated that it was the middle of the night in Düsseldorf. It would have to wait until morning.

At 7:30 a.m. the next morning, I place an international call. My looming question is, Why did this German woman contact me? Dialing, I hope I heard the recorded information correctly. To my surprise, the call connects immediately.

Hearing the excitement in the voice at the other end with her words of greeting, one would think making contact with me was as exciting as striking gold. Her voice continues to express enthusiasm at having successfully tracked me down over a distance spanning four thousand miles.

Hildegard Jakobs,
Director,
The Memorial Center,
Düsseldorf, Germany

The ensuing conversation lasts more than twenty minutes. She explains that approximately ten years before, a woman came to her city's Memorial Center leaving in their possession a translated diary, thinking that it would be appreciated. Further, she explains, the diary had remained untouched in the Center's archives until now.

The Memorial Center, she tells me, is undergoing renovation and will remain closed for the better part of a year. When it reopens my mother's diary is to be the centerpiece exhibit for the opening in 2013. To add to the new exhibit, she says, the Board of Directors wants me to send a copy of my mother's original diary, the German language version, as well as any collection of photos or artifacts still in my possession.

I am excited to hear how enthusiastic she is with just the English translation version of my mother's diary. Immediately after hanging up, I decide to dig deeper into the history of events taking place in Europe as written into my mother's diary's accounts during the years 1939-1941.

Even though the English language diary edition does contain much historical information, I am convinced there is so much more that can be uncovered by careful research. Within the short period of a twenty-minute phone conversation, I was ready to undertake collaboration with Hilde and the Düsseldorf Memorial Museum.

My husband Sandy climbs into our attic to search through contents of a box we had saved containing my mother's photos and an assortment of documents. We want to find as many exhibit worthy pieces as possible to help Ms. Jakobs in her research to illuminate my family. Having previously looked through stored boxes of family history, I have an inkling as to what documents we will find. I am right. We uncover quite a treasure trove of Polish and German records such as work-papers and passports. All are retrieved, then scanned and readied to be sent to the Museum under Hildegard Jakob's supervision.

Over the next few days, we continue to sift through and compile documents, not wanting to leave anything untouched. During this same time, Ms. Jakobs works with speed and enthusiasm delving into reams of documents stored within Düsseldorf city archives. She discovers something important, something of interest she assures us, communicating her find in lightning speed. Germans are serious record-keepers.

She is right. Within the course of forty-eight hours, we

receive information I had no knowledge of concerning my mother and her family. I'm certain the documented information transferred to me has never been previously revealed, nor shared with anyone by my mother. And thus, a family secret comes to light. A secret ultimately playing a most important role in the entire family's survival, having to do with, let us call it, a secret child.

Pieces of information continue to flow to us from Düsseldorf from Hildegard's thorough investigation shedding new light about the family. The first e-mail she sends is about my grandmother, Itta, and my grandfather, Moses, both listed in the city's 1938 directory. Within one directory page, my family's street address was clearly printed. This information was readily available until the family fled Germany after Kristallnacht, November, 1938. City archives also reveal names of all family members. Children's names are listed numerically with a decimal point, as follows:

1.1 Otylia Leah
1.2 Pincus
1.3 Henni

I recognize my mother's brother, Paul and sister, Henni. I grew up in America knowing my Uncle Paul – Pincus, his given name – and my Aunt Henni. They were my mother's only two siblings, or so I thought.

Then, a shock. Sandy's quick recollection motivates him to retrieve a box stored for over thirty-five years. The box, up until now, is thought of as not very important, having no apparent meaning or purpose. Yet, it is stored with all other boxes containing documents for safekeeping. Rifling through its contents, Sandy pulls out a small document. This document, actually a certificate with a handwritten entry, states the name: Carolina Steppel, a child born in 1929.

Carolina!!

A stunning fact my mother never, ever, shared with me – an astonishing disclosure. A family secret. Yet, knowing the way my mother thought about life's challenges, she would have considered this an impediment to her carefully guarded secrets. By Ms. Jakobs sending us information about the unknown child, so much starts to fall into place.

September 2, 2012

Ms. Jakobs continues to unearth family information and streams it to us almost on a daily basis. So knowledgeable is she about Düsseldorf that she can identify the name of a park in an old photograph I scanned and emailed that shows young Leah with friends having a grand time laughing and picnicking. This is an easily identifiable park, where teen-agers would meet on weekends.

Düsseldorf park where teens met.

Portrayed in a two-inch by two-inch black and white photo, Leah could not have been more than sixteen. The scene gives me a sense of comfort, seeing the place where Leah lived prior to final departure from Germany. Examining the old photo closely, I estimate it to be circa 1936.

During a span of ten days, we receive almost no additional communication from Düsseldorf. This lull leads me to anticipate something special is in the making. One afternoon at about 3 p.m. Germany time, I call Hildegard Jakobs anticipating I may receive a gift, a gift in the form of new information. What follows is the essence of the conversation I had that day.

"Today I can report that we have found a number of postcards written by your grandfather, Mojzesz, and sent to a hospital at Schueren, as well as communication from the hospital to your grandparents," Hilde tells me, and continues: "I also received medical records from this hospital, all relevant to the case of a young child, a Steppel family child." The records are written in complex medical terminology, she informs me, and so, "I have not yet been able to translate the information.

Carolina Steppel
B. 12 January, 1929.
D. 1934

Once the uncovered medical information is thoroughly deciphered, the child's medical history will be invaluable to your family for generations to come." She is also investigating the possibility that our family's youngest member, frail and ill

Carolina's birth certificate found by Sandy Barber
amongst old saved documents in the attic of our home.

from birth, never lived within the family home. Ms. Jakobs assures me that all information will be pieced together from postcards and letters as well as the addition of medical records. And this, as promised, she did.

Our Düsseldorf contact believes after the baby's birth, both mother and child remained twelve days in the hospital. Afterwards, the newborn was transferred by my grandmother – her mother – to a facility called Schueren, in Nassau, Germany. The baby Carolina never lived in the house with the other Steppel children. This information is confirmed by correspondence coming from where the child was institutionalized, describing how little Carolina was beginning to walk.

This bit of information, I choose to believe, is one possible reason why my mother never talked about the secret sister, having never lived with the family. My mother was obviously aware of her mother's pregnancy (Leah was 9 years old at the time) and that a birth had definitely taken place. There's a strong possibility that events after the baby's birth may never have been discussed with the other children, and that details were never revealed, and perhaps, unfortunately, forgotten over time. Until, perhaps, when the family was informed that the infant died while still under confinement within the Schueren hospital. With knowledge of the passing of the fourth family child, I believe my mother was determined to preserve, throughout her life, the existence of a long lost baby sister. Carolina's life was undeniably proven by the existence of the birth certificate. I sigh, thinking about all this. Perhaps it was all for the best, a symbol of German stoic behavior, both caring and brave. Still, I wonder, looking back as to how it was all handled, whether it was an expected remnant of the way life was during a post-Victorian era. Beyond receiving all of this important information about Carolina, specifically hospital records, I now have in my possession the only existing photo of the youngster, my aunt. Looking at the photograph, it's easy to see a sweet toddler.

The trail of information continues when a final medical document is sent to me. Difficult as the disclosure is, I'm happy and grateful for it. Now I know how old Carolina was when she died and why she lived outside the family home for the entirety of her short life. First, Carolina only reached the age of four when passing away. And second, this little girl was institutionalized due to an unfortunate heart birth defect. Gazing at her picture, I know immediately that she was, as described during that time, a mongoloid. Today, we

Journal
September 10, 2012

Jacob Meyer Dzikansky,
Lithuania,
circa 1932,
20 years old

While in the midst of researching my mother's history, I remember that today would have been my father's birthday. Thinking about him, I often wonder how my mother was able to acclimate to her new country, finding time to meet a gentlemen, my father. During her first few years in America, she started to learn a skill, specifically in the vocation of jewelry-making, eventually mastering

the art. All during the first few years in America, mother told me she worked constantly to pay for her younger sister Henni's tuition costs to attend art school. Yet, even with this responsibility, she appeared to enjoy herself, finding both time and inclination to enter and win a beauty pageant in Atlantic City.

Leah, a beauty pageant winner, Atlantic City, New Jersey (perhaps 1945)

address this genetic birth defect as Down Syndrome.

Perhaps the multiple physical and cognitive disabilities accompanying the defect were so extensive, she required 'round the clock care within a medical facility rather than living at home with family.

Ironically, the passing of little four-year-old Carolina wiped away any thoughts the family may have harbored to remain in Germany after Hitler's rise to power and growing Jewish onslaught.

May 1984 – The Discovery

She died so young. You, dear reader, ask me who, and I will tell you in my own way. Although I was now married and thirty-five years of age, I, as her daughter, felt the heavy sadness of loss. To me, the reality of my mother's death overwhelmed my thoughts, my emotions, my very soul plunged within deep bereavement and separation – a sense of abandonment – a child to a mother's loss having occurred several years prior. My heart was empty now that my father also succumbed to death eighteen months after my mother. Both my parents were gone, their presence no longer filling our family home. Hollow, lifeless remnants, is how I described it. Wandering through the house stung my heart with emptiness and a part of me fought the urge to close the door and walk away, never to return. But no, that was impossible. The reality of my mother's death followed shortly by my father's departure, washed over me. I wanted to hold on to fraying fragments of a relationship connecting me intensely to my departed mother.

I could not flee, I could not abandon whatever was left of her. Perhaps, I thought, this will be my final visit home clinging to remnants of my mother's and now my father's passing. Standing in the doorway of my parents' bedroom, equal parts of sadness and love wrapped arms around me. I peered at the shared bed, neatly made as always, in the dim glow of a single end table lamp standing soldier-like in appearance. Staring into its yellow glow for endless minutes, my mind drifted to hours earlier.

My younger brother Mark, only 32, his image clear in my mind's eye, possessed good looks beneath a head of hippie length wavy dark hair. But his most distinguished feature: movie star eyes like Paul Newman's, piercing blue and crystal clear. And a booming voice, like that of a Barrett Jackson auctioneer, easily commanding a room full of people. There, in my parents' dining room, my brother had taken command. He invited a sizable crowd, a gathering of former Yeshiva classmates prepared to participate in a minyan followed by the Kaddish for our Father.

I picture him in vivid memory, saying to myself, "Mark's true everlasting persona rings clear holding an invisible microphone."

35

He speaks, his voice thundering:

"'If you promise to say Kaddish for my parents on Yom Kippur, one of you,'" pointing his finger, "'will be honored with this beautiful dining room set," and he sweeps his hand across the table's length, "'once belonging to the infamous gangster Bugsy Siegel.'" Mark was doing what he knew instinctively our parents would appreciate, perpetuating our loved ones' memories with recitation of Kaddish. Through it all, his energy was unrelenting and his emotion was pushed aside and covered over.

That was my brother, Mark, having arrived earlier in the day, flying to New York immediately after hearing of our father's passing. Enduring an eleven hour ELAL flight from Jerusalem, leaving behind family and work responsibilities. But as quickly as he arrived, he immediately departed after all guests had left, catching the next available flight back to his home in Kiryat Ono, Israel. Considered a "super nurse" in Jerusalem, he was the person in charge of the ER triage in the intense environment of Shaare Tzedek Hospital. The memory of Mark's presence and theatrical performance faded as quickly as my feeling of loss returned.

Once again finding myself alone in the house, my feet trudged forward and I enter my parents' bedroom. Eyes moist with tears focused on a single ornate lamp crowned by a beige shade. Its soft yellow glow above my mother's night table guided me inward.

My hands began to tremble as I moved closer. Some unexplainable force drew me toward the end table, its single drawer a hallowed resting place within which lay, I would soon discover, the secret. The drawer slid open grudgingly and the lamplight exposed a secretary pouch, red in color, within which I found undisclosed details of family history.

The red
'secretary'
and the
contents
Mother
never shared.

Its contents went undisturbed long through my childhood
and well into adulthood.

A questioning thought ping-ponged across my mind.

Perhaps, I wanted to believe, had Mother lived longer,
she might have shared her secrets with me, but only when
she felt the time was right. This, I rationalized. But revelation
never occurred. Secrets of the diaries were never spoken
about. Now, within the moment, trembling fingers lifted out
two thin hardcover books recognizable as diaries. Diaries, I
would soon discover, written totally in German.

"Yes," I whispered to myself. Family secrets resting in
my hands were light years away from comprehension. Yet,
I was determined to unveil what had been hidden from
me. I desired to know, but feared what I might discover.
Written entirely in my mother's native language, mastery
for understanding remained elusive. Secrets to be unlocked
required the key of translation. Within the last few minutes,
yes, I alone attempted to climb the Mt. Everest of family
secrets, but still its summit would be unconquered with its
potentially shocking truths. Revelations would take time to
unfold.

Curious and impulsive, I leafed through one page after

Buried on Har Hamenuchot in Jerusalem:
Rabbi Jacob Meyer Dykan (1912-1984)
Leah Dykan (1920-1982)

another. The dim light cast by the lamp nonetheless acted as a beacon, prodding me to face the difficult questions running across my mind.

What secrets did Leah, my mother, write within the pages of these two thin little diary books? I glanced at dates, easily understandable. The first was penned January, 1939.

What had she written about? my curious mind asked over and over. More questions persisted.

Why had she never shared diary contents with me?

What are all the addresses in the back of one book?

There were no answers, no immediate revelations, no easing of long hidden truths. All remained a mystery. Did I really want to know? Perhaps. Once I returned to Maryland with the protective red secretary pouch holding two diaries, I placed it in my night table drawer where it remained untouched for the next ten years.

During this decade-long period following first my mother and then my father's death, I had accompanied Dad's remains to

38

Israel where he was to be buried beside his wife. After burial in Israel, I remained a month after Shiva and until dad's matzava, memorial stone, was finally erected.

More years flew by. In 1995, when news indicated impending approval of a museum to document the Holocaust in Washington, D.C., I scheduled a meeting with the head curator. I will never forget going through the corridors of offices, seeing walls and walls of photos, and boxes of possessions and shoes, lots and lots of shoes. There were researchers working on documents, sifting through the only remains of a once-proud European Jew. The curator and I spent hours going through my parent's diaries, passports and documents.

"We are very interested in your mother's account," she said. "But until the permanent displays for the future Holocaust museum have been determined, we would put her possessions in our archives to be used for future exhibits." If I agreed to give the diaries and documents to the museum, they would become the property of the United States government. He ended with, "You can view your mother's diaries at anytime. Just call and make an appointment." I was not ready to turn over my mother's unknown legacy, so upon returning home, I put everything back in the night table drawer.

Shortly afterward, I felt emotionally strong enough to work with a gentleman of Polish/German descent, Rabbi Weiner, who was able to complete a German to English translation. With his help, Leah's words came to light. A young woman, barely nineteen years of age, thoughtfully described by the translator as a clever, tenacious, risk-taking, and courageous woman. Her faith boundless, attributing to her survival by escaping Nazi-occupied Europe with the help of her 'Lucky Star' and deep belief in G-d.

From Paris To Bordeaux

June 24, 2017

*O*ur taxi whizzes us beyond the airport into the city of Bordeaux, France. Excitement and curiosity run through my mind – what sights, what memories would come to our attention? Gazing through our transport's window, landmarks at first mean nothing, registering no link to my mother's diary descriptions of this French city. Bordeaux's modern appearance differs widely from my expectations – at least for the moment.

We arrive at our first destination, the Mercure Hotel. Before stepping from the taxi, I look out, noticing our hotel is tucked between modern office buildings off a main avenue. It is a small, modern structure within Bordeaux's historical downtown area. Looking at its façade, I feel a bit off kilter, a sense of being transported backward in time. A momentary sensory time warp experience.

After handing over passports at the front desk we finished with registration. Sandy and I have an opportunity to walk several blocks surrounding the area before returning to the hotel, ready to meet fellow travelers for dinner. With warm anticipation, we begin the process of becoming acquainted with other members of the group. Soon, we are to become a cohesive gathering, pursuing an important mission, in which we each become immersed in memories of a very personal experience.

For this day, June 24, 2017, is the first step of an enlightening, spellbinding undertaking, the beginning of a personal quest to follow my mother's long ago journey.

During our brief walk before dinner and meeting the others, I carry my mother's precious diaries, absorbing sights carefully penned, which described Bordeaux in the year 1940. In stark contrast to my mother's descriptions of bustling, harried multitudes of refugees pouring through this city, Bordeaux, now, before my eyes, appears tranquil within this second decade of the twenty-first century.

We have time to venture down one of the city's main boulevards, passing 19th and 20th century buildings, elegant four- and five-story sizable limestone residences, each bearing a small but noticeable brass plaque.

I wonder, "What is inscribed on each plaque – is it something that happened during the turbulence of WWII?"

The further we walk, the more I grow aware that my pace is easing into slow-motion rhythm. This awareness, this feeling becomes more frequent throughout my journey, enabling me to absorb sights and sounds imbued with the past. I sense mother's presence within my own footsteps bringing me, somehow, closer to her, knowing she walked these same streets, passed these same buildings. Are these sensory memories real, or is it just my imagination? I feel closer and closer to my mother's footsteps, her presence walking in lockstep with mine. Beginning in Bordeaux, my mother's experiences, her movement through the countries, become stronger with each step along our parallel journey, immersing me deeper and deeper within Leah's diary account.

Adding to the dynamic of insight and understanding, members of the Sousa Mendes Foundation soon embrace us with details as they join our 28-member group for the entirety of our journey. I know I need to "steel" myself with patience and calm, realizing for the first time in my life, I truly walked in my mother's footsteps!

By late afternoon on that first day in Bordeaux, we return to the Mercure Hotel. My anticipation and excitement abounds with thoughts about everything coming next. Our first Meet and Greet takes place in a private room within our hotel. So many new people to meet and chat with about the momentous journey ahead. Conversations erupt in every corner, in every space within the comfort of the small meeting room. I hear passionate talk among the group. We form a circle, introduce ourselves and share information, explaining who within our families were visa recipients arranged by the righteous gentleman, Aristides de Sousa Mendes. Everyone in the group, I'm sure, is honored to speak the name of Sousa Mendes and his noble act of kindness and generosity. These descendants have the opportunity to explain what they hope to achieve along the journey connected to events played out seven decades before. Most are second- or third-generation relatives of Sousa Mendes' original visa recipients. Without precious Portuguese visas, no escape would have been possible.

The crowd hushes with two important introductions. First is Gerald Mendes, the grandson of Sousa Mendes. He announces his intention to accompany the group throughout most of the journey.

Next, Dr. Olivia Mattis, founder and now president and COO of the Sousa Mendes Foundation, is introduced. She is a musicologist, while devoting much of her time to raising funds for The Foundation's work and mission. Having conducted previous journeys, Olivia's tantamount objective is to provide extensive details about a historically difficult journey, one where life and death hung in the balance as thousands of refugees streamed along dusty, crammed roads, by any means of transportation. Thousands pushed themselves westward, then south, crossing Spain then into Portugal. Dr. Mattis provides details of their journey, including towns and places traversed. She makes every effort to tell us about geographic details where our relatives passed through for a day, a night, a week, along their road to freedom.

Olivia is connected to us through more than just our trip, however. Twelve members of her paternal family were also rescued by Aristides de Sousa Mendes.

Dr. Olivia Mattis,
President and COO
of the Sousa Mendes
Foundation

Her family escaped from Belgium in 1940, and during this time of crisis Olivia's mother survived the war as a hidden child remaining in Belgium. She also speaks of her maternal grandparents, organizers of Belgium's Jewish Resistance. She organizes high-profile international conferences and music festivals, receiving media coverage from Good Morning America and The New York Times. In addition, she's contributing editor to the Jewish Genealogy and Family History Journal, Avotaynu Online and author of Sousa Mendes' List – The Search For Survivors.

After introductions and highlights of coming events, a sense of relief washes over me. Yet, within the joy of meeting and getting to know fellow travelers, I feel underlying tension connected to the anticipated journey.

Finally, dinner is announced, prompting participants to

stream into the hotel's Le Parvis restaurant. Seated around a circular table, I recall a number of conversations pulling me closer to particular group members. A level of comfort quietly connects me to several. One is a beautiful eighty-year-old Parisian artist, Alexandra Grieg, and another, the most senior traveler, a ninety-four year old female, Lissy Jarvik, M.D., Ph.D., the oldest direct visa recipient on our journey.

"I was a recipient of a Sousa Mendes visa," she tells us. "Otherwise, I wouldn't be here." Jarvik was just sixteen when her Jewish family fled their home in the Netherlands in 1940. She has come back to France today with her son, Dr. Jerry Jarvik, and two college-age granddaughters, Ella and Leah.

Lissy speaks his name, Sousa Mendes, many times over dinner conversations. This is her third journey with The Foundation and I would later observe that Lissy is a veritable rock-star when we visit our savior's home and the middle school bearing his name.

Aristides de Sousa Mendes

I muse often during the journey about each of my companions – a close-knit group bearing common bonds and common scars. We, the lucky ones, descendants, must always remember, never forgetting, that none of us, nor our descendants, would exist without the goodness and courage of the Portuguese diplomat.

Aristides de Sousa Mendes started his career in 1910 with postings in British Guiana, Galicia, Poland and Zanzibar. Promoted to Consul General in 1918, he held positions in Antwerp, and San Francisco, and finally Bordeaux, France when World War II broke out. By June of 1940, tens of thousands of European refugees began flocking to Bordeaux,

44

France, including the Steppel family, in advance of Nazi armies. Refugees had one objective – acquiring a visa to cross through Spain. These desperate masses, most often, had no choice but to sleep in railway cars, public parks, and often on the streets. Many consulates were shutting their doors and denying visas. When Paris was captured, the French government moved to Bordeaux, becoming France's de facto capital. Due to the German army's capture of Paris, the Steppel family followed suit, fleeing to Bordeaux. They had already been on the road for over a year.

Aristides de Sousa Mendes,
Portuguese Consul General in Bordeaux

Diplomat Sousa Mendes was the organizer of what is most likely the largest rescue operation during the Holocaust. Operating in Bordeaux during the hours immediately following the German invasion, tens of thousands of refugees swarmed toward Southern France hoping to gain safety, making their way into Spain to find a haven in a country still accepting refugees. Unfortunately, the government of Portugal responded to the refugee crisis with a document called Circular 14, explicitly instructing diplomats not to issue visas and shutting down its immigration process.

45

Entry was prohibited at the very moment when a stamp in a passport made all the difference between life and death.

The situation weighed on the conscience of Sousa Mendes, who was a devout Catholic. It is at this point in time he makes the acquaintance of Rabbi Chaim Kruger, a refugee from Poland. Each deeply religious in their own faith, they formed a deep friendship.

Aristides offered to issue Kruger and his immediate family visas, but the Rabbi declined, saying, "It is not only for me, but for all the refugees gathering outside the consulate."

Having witnessed the horrors of the Jews round up in Poland, the rabbi painted a picture that preyed on Aristides' Catholic heart and mind. On June 15, 1940, he was resolute, and began the process of granting visas to each and every refugee regardless of race, creed, or religion. Meanwhile throngs of refugees had gathered on a staircase leading to his consulate office, afraid if they left they could lose their place in line.

Operating in explicit defiance of his Foreign Office's instruction, Sousa Mendes and his assistant Jose Seabra, counselor secretary, responded to desperate people by issuing visas. With two of his sons, he worked day and night, between June 15 and June 22, issuing thousands of visas before collapsing from exhaustion.

Most of the people rescued were ordinary men, women and children facing persecution. Had they not been issued visas, all would have been eventually transported to death camps established in German-occupied Poland. Among those rescued by Sousa Mendes were fine arts painter Salvador Dali and Hans and Margret Rey, better known as the authors of Curious George.

Mendes' contemporaries regarded him as a rogue

diplomat flooding his country with unwanted, dependent people unable to care for themselves. Supporting the issuance of Circular 14, the Portuguese government at the time was fearful Nazi agents were among the refugees bringing venomous racism and anti-Semitism, helping to undermine Portugal's neutrality. In spite of unsubstantiated fears, the true picture of history portrayed Sousa Mendes as a man of nobility who saved thousands of men, women and children. His motives were clear. He saw desperation of the oppressed and inhumanity closing off havens for rescue – and he acted.

As a result, the Portuguese Foreign office caught wind of his efforts and recalled him home. Put on trial in Portugal for disobedience, he was stripped of all titles and disgraced. Unable to support his large family during the next quarter century, he lost their home, in Cabana de Veriato, and he died as a penniless nonperson in 1954.

Reflecting on Sousa Mendes' downfall, Olivia Mattis, whose father was among those rescued in 1940 said, "Most good people are risk adverse. This government official wasn't."

"Without dictates of my faith, I stand with God against man rather than man against God," Sousa Mendes said.

"It's not that he knew he was saving people from genocide," said Edna Friedberg, a historian at the U.S. Holocaust Memorial Museum. "He was saving people from persecution, and for him, that was enough."

In what the historian Yehuda Bauer described as "Perhaps the largest rescue action by a single individual during the Holocaust" – larger even than the famous intervention by Schindler – he offered indiscriminate assistance to tens of thousands.

His friendship with Chaim Kruger, a Chassidic Polish Rabbi who fled Belgium for France – and refused to accept a visa from Sousa Mendes, unless he did the same for the Jews amassed on the streets and parks of Bordeaux – is attributed to have been the turning point.

Rabbi Chaim Kruger with Sousa Mendes.

Many of those he rescued went on to lead prominent lives in the United States and elsewhere. The extended family of Parisian gallery owner Paul Rosenberg, a legendary dealer of Picasso, Braque, and Matisse, escaped to New York thanks to the seventeen visas issued to him and his family by Sousa Mendes in the summer of 1940. His son, Alexandre, joined the free French Forces. Marianne Rosenberg, his daughter, had many a story to tell. She is for me a "Woman in Gold," traveling the world, fighting to retrieve many of her grandfather's plundered masterpieces.

"You have to ask yourself whether you would make the same choice," said Jerry Jarvik, M.D., accompanying his mother, Lissy Jarvik, M.D., Ph.D. age ninety-three, who received a Sousa Mendes transit visa when she was sixteen.

"Would I sacrifice the future of these two?" he said, gesturing at his two daughters.

Based on details related to our group, the old Portuguese embassy in Bordeaux became a most important location to visit along our journey.

Leah Steppel, 19, in Antwerp, 1939.
Jewish organization leader, visionary.

Our first official photo taken at the memorial bust
of Aristides de Sousa Mendes in Bordeaux. I am with Sandy,
on the right, fourth in from the memorial.

Paul Rosenberg great Parisian art empresario, whose granddaughter, Marianne, was among the group.

Above: Standing in front of Andy Warhol's portrait is Ina Ginsberg, a visa recipient, Washington, D.C. doyenne and arts patron, whose son, Mark, was on the journey. *Right*: Lissy Jarvik, M.D., Ph.D., pioneer in the field of neuropsychogeriatrics, a direct visa recipient, was our group's senior member.

During the group's first dinner assembly, we discuss the many sites to be visited, highlighted by testimonials.

Dr. Mattis chooses the Great Bordeaux Synagogue as part of the following day's agenda. An important and fitting site for the group, though it is not by chance that Dr. Mattis chooses the Grande Synagogue – she has me in mind. I had sent her a copy of my mother's diary and specific entries convinced her that certain locations would be significant, especially to me.

Given advanced notice, I prepared short testimonial talks for the group. Successfully received, I was asked to present twice more.

Spare time during connecting bus rides afforded opportunity to reflect upon what I would say. I had brought with me copies of my mother's photos and passports adding a more dynamic, realistic aspect to my presentations.

Bordeaux-The Stone Bridge

June 25, 2017

Our group moves toward the Esplanade de Quinconces, one of the most photographed sites in the city and the most emblematic of the French Revolution in Bordeaux with the famous monument built for the Girondins. Located on the river, this 12-hectare square is the largest in Europe. On a grand scale, at the end of the square, stands an enormous fountain displaying many intricate metal wrought figurines. Our guide tells us that during the Nazis' march through France, they commandeered all metal statues to be melted down for armaments. In defiance, French resistance groups

51

painstakingly took the fountain apart, hiding pieces in barns throughout the countryside. To say this was a jigsaw puzzle on a grand scale is an understatement. It was not until the early 1980s that all disassembled pieces were found and reassembled.

We stand before this amazing fountain and I wonder what my nineteen-year-old mother saw seventy-seven years into the past. Did she see it in its full form glory? Did she witness the fountain hastily dismantled or was it but an empty space where the fountain once existed? Next I wonder: Did she stand alone at this site? If so, where were her siblings, her parents? Were family members camped out on this very space next to the river surrounded by hordes of other refugees?

The fountain in Bordeaux, dismantled before the Nazis could get to it, was then painstakingly put back together.

Lithograph of the masses at Stone Bridge,
1940, Bordeaux

The Stone Bridge present day

Perhaps my mind plays tricks, but I allow myself imagery of footstep impressions made by my mother upon this historical spot on French soil. I think back to a photo I possess of the fountain restored with its surrounding grounds. With each footstep I take following Otylia-Leah Steppel's journey, I truly believe I move closer toward a more poignant picture of my mother. Imagining the scene

53

decades ago, she sits beside the city's riverside close to the monument, contemplating next steps along her journey of freedom – a journey my footsteps continue to follow.

From the Esplanade de Quinconces vantage point, I gaze, perhaps a bit mesmerized, upon The Stone Bridge, a historical site spanning the Garonne River. I'm certain that here, in 1940, upon this very stone causeway, Leah and her immediate family crossed over among masses of other refugees. I picture in my mind's eye the choked passageway teaming with desperate people. The reality of mother's wartime existence materializes before my eyes, yet again. I stand stiff and resolute. I shudder from chills as I build more of a connecting bridge between mother and me. I walk in my mother's footsteps

The imminent fall of France to fast-approaching German troops made it clear Paris would soon be occupied.
Therefore, Portuguese government workers operating in the Paris Portuguese embassy, with great haste, were transferred to the French city of Bordeaux.
Here, a brownstone residence was converted into a de facto "official," yet temporary, embassy.

The Grande Bordeaux Synagogue

June 26, 2017

I think to myself, "Had Leah heard about the efforts of a Portuguese diplomat, a miracle worker, motivating her to follow hordes of European refugees working their way to the temporary embassy in Bordeaux? Or, did Leah just happen upon the scene where thousands gathered around the consulate, hoping to gain a turn at presenting themselves to Aristides de Sousa Mendes and his assistant, Jose Seabres?"

My journey of 2017 continues. After a superb continental style breakfast, including croissants and espresso, we board our tour bus for the short ride to the Grande Synagogue of Bordeaux. I am familiar with its location because my mother clearly writes about walking into this synagogue after she and her family arrive in Bordeaux. Mother's diary entry date, and her signed and dated visa, prove she was there between June 17-20, 1940.

The closest our tour bus driver can park is a block from the synagogue, requiring us to approach the synagogue on foot. Roads in this city are narrow but also, we are informed, security precautions require it. Its edifice appears quite grand. Standing guard by the front entrance is a resolute, serious looking young soldier, his weapon held fixed in his hands. Security measures also require the exterior of this magnificent house of worship to be surrounded by a tall iron fence. Immediately upon entering, one sees a wall dedicated to fallen French heroes who fought in two World Wars. Walking further inside, I clutch my mother's diary as well as other documents I'm accustomed to carrying. I always want to be prepared to share them with whomever might be interested.

While walking through the interior, I think about the content and tone of my testimonial to be presented shortly within this grand house of worship. The synagogue president and Olivia decide on the Chapel for presentations by myself and Barbara Berger Opotowsky. Following a short talk by the congregation's president and a tour of the building, it is

"After a long journey we arrived in Bordeaux, completely broken and dead tired. We did not know where to go. We were desperate. The men were allowed to stay overnight in the synagogue. The place was everything else but hygienic and clean. For the women staying there was completely impossible.

In the evening many members came to the synagogue. One of them invited me to sleep at her house until we could find lodging. It was her son (who liked me). He was very attentive towards me from the first moment he saw me. He was 20 years old and did everything for me. I had only to point out what I wanted. He said he would even 'fall out with his family for me."

my time to speak. I feel overwhelmed and can only hope to hold myself together. My mother's indomitable spirit stands beside me, bolstering my strength and ability to present. The centerpiece of my talk centers on recollections of Leah and her family and how they made their way to this city. I also include a diary entry describing a proposal of marriage she received while temporarily living in a Bordeaux residence. Wow! Even within all the turmoil of escape, a flower of romance blossomed, at least temporarily. This was my first presentation to our group and happily, I received warm, lovely applause at its conclusion. The finale of our group's visit to the Grande Bordeaux Synagogue includes a sumptuous lunch.

The fully restored Grande Synagogue
of Bordeaux.

Rebecca's
testimonial in the
Chapel of the
Synagogue.

The synagogue undergoes a modern-day facelift.

Bordeaux Mysteries Unraveled

June 26, 2017

After lunch, I am astonished when Aristides' grandson, Gerald, approaches, explaining that residence locations listed in the back of my mother's diary, pertaining to people then living in Bordeaux, were only a five- to ten-minute walk from the Grande Synagogue. Not surprisingly, quite a few from our group jump at the opportunity to follow Gerald, Sandy, and me. We set out using a GPS navigating device leading us to the addresses. Never did I imagine that I would actually be able to come in contact with places and possibly people who sheltered my mother so long ago.

Within a few minutes' walk, we arrive at 57 Cours de Victor Hugo, a four-story apartment building. Unfortunately, the entry is locked. Undeterred, we notice a store located next to the building and I inquire with the clerk if he knows a family named Mueller living in one of the apartments next store. No luck! We return to the front of the building, feeling somewhat disappointed. But then, the front door opens and a young woman appears with a cart, prepared to do daily shopping. We ask the same question posed to the store clerk. Again, no luck – she, too, did not know the family. But, all was not in vain. We were able to steal a peek into the building's long front hallway. A hallway through which my mother passed and the building where she temporarily lived provided by the graciousness of a woman named Mueller at the end of June, 1940.

Still hoping to make even more contact with my mother's past, we move on, finding two additional addresses noted in her diary. To preserve the moment, our accompanying photographer snaps photos of Sandy and me standing in front of two other addresses. Excited, and as I recall, breathless, I feel satisfied having been able to find these residences – such a discovery happening in my lifetime!

Leah wrote addresses in the back of her diary, which were, before the journey, a mystery.

Gerald and fellow travelers accompanying us are also happy for me, knowing I continue walking in my mother's footsteps. If nothing else is unveiled during this historical journey, I can honestly say, as my parents did at Passover – Dayenu!

59

Left: 57 Cours Victor Hugo, where Leah was taken in by a woman from the synagogue. *Right:* Found! 5 Rue Beaubadat.

Sandy and Rebecca at 1 Rue Retaillon, the last of three residences where Leah took refuge in Bordeaux.

Bayonne, France

June 27, 2017

Bayonne, a city southwest of Bordeaux located in the Basque Country region of France, borders areas of the Pyrenees Mountains. We arrive and our group is guided to the old Portuguese consulate where Sousa Mendes ordered visas to be issued by vice-consul Manuel de Vieira Braga.

Toward the end of June, 1940, Aristides de Sousa Mendes managed to evacuate his Paris consulate, moving it to Bayonne. His new consulate location was on a small street opposite a cathedral, and from that location, he encountered thousands of desperate people waiting for visas, granting them entrance to Spain. Once in Portugal, seaports along its coast became exit points, with ships able to depart Europe for the Americas, Africa or Palestine, and Haiti.

Standing inside the old Portuguese consulate building, we notice a marble staircase leading up to a second floor. Our guide explains that the entire staircase right up to the entry door supported hundreds of squeezed-together refugees. The diplomat of compassion, Sousa Mendes, was afraid the staircase would collapse under the weight of so many people packed together. Observing the uncertainty of the rickety old wooden staircase, he immediately ordered members of his staff to carry a table into the courtyard where the waiting crowd could at least avoid injury from the over-stressed staircase while diplomatic staff carried out issuing visas indiscriminately.

Looking up and down at the staircase, I feel an urge to grasp the railing and slowly climb the steps. With each step,

I hold the railing tighter, giving me a sensation of connecting with my mother. I envision the jostled desperate masses, Leah among them, and perhaps Ina, Mark's mother, only a few years older, by her side. All day, she describes in her diary, she stood hour after hour refusing to lose her place in line. Stopping midway up the staircase, I felt my mother's discomfort surrounded by a multitude of anxious, strained people. She would not take a step back, she could not take a step forward. She waited, for receiving a visa meant life!

Retreating from the old staircase, I stand in the courtyard sensing a link with my mother, waiting for the precious document granting passage into Spain. Then, my memory reverts back to a diary entry with words referring to "settling other matters." It strikes me she could be so nonchalant, cavalier with an attitude about achieving the next step to freedom. I'm emotionally moved by her tenacity under such stressful conditions and even more so by her focused, determined, independent resolve. Among thousands of others, she persevered alone while parents and siblings waited in Bordeaux, praying for her success.

Sousa Mendes' objective, we learn, was to sign as many documents as fast as possible so refugees could cross the border before German troops arrived, forcing Spanish border guards to close entrance to Irun, Spain. Hearing details of this pivotal day in my mother's life literally took my breath away. She must have felt frantic inside, yet calm on the surface, aware of the ticking clock foretelling the German Army's approach. I reflect upon my young mother's state of mind, sensing she must have cleverly calculated while waiting on the staircase. Deciding to utilize available transportation allowed her to travel back and forth between several French cities during a period of five days and nights. My guess is, she traveled by train, since I observe numerous rail stations passed by our tour bus linking towns and cities. I marvel at every beautifully restored station. Most look straight out of a period movie set, circa World War II, brought back to beautiful, functional modern condition. We eventually visit two of note.

Members of the group along the stairway of the Bayonne makeshift consulate.

Hendaye and Salamanca

June 27, 2017

Today's modern tour buses glide comfortably along well paved roads and highways, significantly reducing travel time. But in 1940, this was not the case. Leah Steppel trudged along her arduous journey of escape mostly on foot – always one step ahead of disaster.

Leading her immediate family, they pushed onward following dusty, crowded country roads filled with fleeing refugees, most afoot, some atop horse-drawn wagons piled high with children and household goods. Day after day, under perilous conditions of war, and all that war brings within its path and within its wrath, the Steppel family marched on. Although Leah's words clearly illustrate strong moments of faith in her use of G-d Almighty, and something she calls her "Lucky Star," as I learn from our guide and fellow travelers, this was a terrible ordeal, with constant stumbling blocks and nothing promised for their future.

In 2017, our group travels by modern tour bus from Bordeaux, France to Bayonne, France, then on to Hendaye – a one- and a half-hour ride. Arriving in Hendaye, on June 27, 2017, our intention is to walk across the "Freedom Bridge" linking France to Spain, but this is impossible since the bridge is closed for repairs. Without this memorable crossing, our agenda calls for a recitation of testimonials followed by a meeting with the town's mayor, journalists and other government personnel. After these ceremonial meetings, we remain only a short time, then push on to Salamanca, Spain.

It is here, I note on this very spot, our group crosses the

border just as Leah had seventy-seven years before.

September, 1940

"I arrived at Hendaye (in the Pyrenees'
region of France) dead tired. There I
settled the remaining formalities, (and)
we readied ourselves to cross the border.
After a long wait at the French/Spanish
border, we came to Irun. Immediately
upon entering this border town we saw
what terrible results Spain had suffered from its long
civil war. Most of the city was in ruins! Later, when we
traveled in a slow train through Spain we saw what
kind of poverty (and) destruction had befallen the
country. This once beautiful, flourishing, (and) rich
land was in shambles. War destroys everything. Why
don't foolish people understand that one can only lose;
no one wins by war."

Touring Salamanca with its beautiful scenery, we soon
come upon its grand university, the jewel of the city. Founded
in 1134, the university is a walk back within medieval history.

Leah, in her diary, refers to Spain in "tatters" due to their
recent Civil War. Her description is in stark contrast to what
we see today in this beautiful city. We stay overnight at the
Abba Francesca Hotel and spend a delightful evening on our
own.

Rebecca at Salamanca Square, 2017

Salamanca Square, 1940

Stepping From Salamanca, Spain, Into Portugal

June 28, 2017

We thoroughly enjoy our first evening in Salamanca as well as the following morning. After breakfast, I wander around since we have free time and I think about where Leah may have slept in this war torn city back in 1940.

Later that morning, we travel to the important border

town of Vilar Formoso where refugees were warmly welcomed during the tumult of the early '40s. Today, traffic flows smoothly between Spanish and Portuguese borders. But in 1940, visas were strictly required in order to cross. With official stamped visas, Leah and her family passed from Spain to Portugal.

Our first stop in Portugal is a train station, where most certainly Leah and the entire Steppel family arrived. I marvel at the beauty of this train station with its blue and white porcelain tile murals, a signature Portuguese style. The station itself is exactly as it had been in 1940, albeit returned to its original grand state. Looking about the station's many artistic touches, my mind wanders, anticipating my second testimonial to be delivered to our group in Vilar Formosa. I am confident and thoroughly prepared.

Still within sight of the train station, I look toward the near distance recognizing a construction site. I am told this is the future home of the Frontier of Peace Refugees Memorial Museum, dedicated in part to Aristides' efforts of heroism. The museum's focus would also be to illuminate the many Portuguese towns that played an important role housing refugees, including Leah Steppel. I am relieved my young mother was now in Portugal and I, there with her in spirit, as well. I remember taking a deep breath, feeling her great burden lift, having led her family to safety, crossing through France and Spain. In solidarity with my mother, I too feel a lifting of pain and worry once having crossed into Portugal.

After a particularly delicious lunch, almost a feast, we move to the museum's construction site where we are to be introduced to quite a few personalities: the museum architect, Luisa Marques; the historical consultant, Margarida Ramalho; the mayor, a journalist, and a photographer. Many townspeople are also in attendance. The private viewing of the still unfinished museum is led by its chief architect. The group is presented with a special tour that is far beyond expectation. Provided with hard hats, we are led through the still-under-construction historical museum. Exhibits will include statements of generosity from people living within surrounding towns of Curia and Porto. These townspeople provided refugee families, including the Steppels, with food, shelter and, most of all, hope.

Of greatest significance, the new museum is to be dedicated to Aristides de Sousa Mendes for the life-saving help provided to tens of thousands. The Foundation, in his honor, features photo images of families receiving visas from the great man along with artifacts such as passports, visas, and an original doll exhibit. Artifacts pertaining to one very special refugee, my mother, are unfortunately not going to be part of the initial exhibit once the museum officially opens. In spite of this, I leave copies of Steppel family documents and a few small remembrances brought with me, including photographs taken by a Spanish journalist who had greeted and accompanied us during part of the journey. This gracious journalist later wrote a splendid article prominently featuring Leah's photos, as well as me in a hard hat.

Now safely ensconced within Portugal, I feel a calming affect overcoming both my mother and myself. Again, I say, we truly walk closer together in her footsteps.

Clockwise from top: Walking through the then incomplete
Frontier of Peace Museum; Rebecca with the Mayor
of Vilar Formoso, Portugal;
Marianne Rosenberg and Rebecca
at the construction site;
Vilar Formoso train station.

Above: Leah's stamped visa at the border town
of Vilar Formoso, Portugal.
Below: The President,
Marcelo Rebelo de Sousa (no relation)
at the opening of Frontier of Peace Museum,
one month after our tour.

Cabanas de Viriato: Casa do Passal

June 29, 2017

Today we travel one and a half hours, distancing ourselves from our visit to the Frontier of Peace Refugees Memorial Museum. Our tour bus glides quietly along toward our next destination, and I find myself within a relaxed state of contemplation. Travel time is most welcome, as it helps to separate us from an emotionally charged visit to the museum. Should I return someday, or if future descendants choose to, one will see my mother's name engraved upon magnificent 30-inch by 30-inch marble blocks forming a wall in honor of refugees. Along the way, I am informed the museum we just left is scheduled to officially open one short month after our visit. (*See photos on page 69.*)

Our bus slows as we approach our next destination – a visit to the deeply rooted origins of Aristides de Sousa Mendes. Our destination, Viseu, a Portuguese municipality and a visit to Cabanas de Viriato, hometown to the Sousa Mendes family. Again, I remind myself, this man gave up his diplomatic standing, and his wealth, effecting his family's standard of living for the well-being of my mother and tens of thousands of other desperate refugees.

Casa do Passal is the official name given to the Aristides' home located in North Central Portugal. Built in the 19th century, it functioned as his primary residence for the family until the property was forfeited to a bank in the 1950s. This was so unfortunate to both the house and the family as it remained unoccupied for decades, sorely deteriorating to the point where repair required structural as well as extensive

71

interior renovation. Fortunately, at the very beginning of the twenty-first century, the property and acreage were re-acquired, and now it's the descendants' intention to repair the house and transform it into a memorial museum perpetuating the memory of Aristides de Sousa Mendes. Support for the cause to honor and memorialize the savior came from around the world, including from Jewish and Portuguese communities all eager to see the realization of this longstanding indomitable goal fulfilled. A statement from The Foundation corroborates this dream – now a goal.

Approaching the property by bus, I wonder how I will react walking about the grounds and finally entering the home. The bus slows, traveling cautiously along a narrow banked and hilly road, climbing closer to the property. Until now, the man, Sousa Mendes, is a compilation of historical facts, a legend in word and deed and there exists in my mind a certain distance from him as a flesh and blood person. About to enter his former home, I wonder if seeing how and where he lived could, or would, reveal a more human perception.

Within this train of thought, could a similarity be drawn to my mother? Remembering intricate, revealing details penned within two diaries and photos of her displayed in an album I brought along, again strengthened a connection with my mother as both Sousa Mendes and Leah were similarly involved in crisis situations. Threads of people's lives, even though they may be very different could be similarly connected. Refocusing my thoughts, I am ready to enter the former world of Sousa Mendes.

Previously, my journeying companions and I had been shown photos of the sorrowful dilapidated condition of his estate. When the bus finally rolls up in front of the sprawling home, I am immediately stunned by such a visually beautiful sight. The house – truly a mansion – was not a modest home by any stretch of the imagination. Just the opposite. It is three stories high, consisting of at least 12,000 square feet of living space. Fourteen children once lived there with parents and attendants at some point in time.

Our group gathers, listening to the owner of a company who worked the bones of "Passal." Photos existed of the home before its decline, enabling this gentleman to cast molds and reproduce colors for trim on the main house. Now restored, the exterior renovation is absolutely breathtaking. The completely renovated and re-painted Beaux Arts exterior and surrounding grounds are all beautifully landscaped. An ornate facade trimmed with gilded embellishments recreate original architecture. A huge banner depicting Sousa Mendes, during the height of his diplomatic years, is affixed to the left front section of the home, so there is no question as to the former owner. We climb twenty steps, then stand on an elevated exterior landing because the building is graded quite a bit higher than the road below. I'm guessing now, but I believe this noble house could be observed for miles around due its lofty elevation within the very center of the town. Near us, within the property's gate, stands an imposing granite statue, do Cristo-Rei, which has been on the grounds since 1933. Once again, I think of the Righteous Gentile.

We're informed the building itself is closed to the public, except we are granted special privileges to enter, just as with the Frontier of Peace Museum in Vilar Formoso. But because of safety reasons, we're told to remain on the main level. We enter through enormous doors. An eye-opening sight greets me. The entire interior's main floor space was gutted down to the exterior walls while all the floors remain as unfinished cement. No interior doors are hung, yet all windows had been replaced, protecting the home's interior from the elements. I marvel at these beautiful new windows, all reproduced in Beaux Art style. In front of me, a two-story foyer boasts a ten-foot wide sweeping center staircase similarly portrayed in many Hollywood era movies of the 30s and 40s. Breathtaking in its elegance! After twenty or so steps, there is a large landing with the staircase splitting left and right. An entire bank of stained glass panels hangs above the landing, a few remarkably still in good condition. When the sun peeks from behind occasional clouds, we see how ten coordinated stained-glass panels produce a dazzling spectacle when sunlight strikes it just right. Also, I can imagine Sousa Mendes' children running up and down the stairs and the kind of trouble they could find themselves in with these precious panels.

The 'Passal' as the home was lovingly called, was unfortunately mortgaged in the 1940s, along with plots of land belonging to the estate, in order to help support his children after ruination caused by the Portuguese government, and thus, the nobility of his diplomatic status was harshly removed and to make matters worse, his wife died in 1948, and by 1949, many of his children emigrated from Portugal. The family in ruins, a direct result of his humanitarian beliefs and actions.

Previously within an environment of elegant living, security and comfort, I believe Aristides thought about the contrast of his life compared to thousands of displaced, rag-tag refugees flooding into Portugal. Rapidly occurring events taking place throughout Western Europe must have roiled his sensibilities, which were then crushed beneath the jack boots of advancing Nazi armies. Perhaps his life style contrasting so sharply with those on the run helped clarify his perception of events. Clarification catapulted into action for humanitarian reasons. I wonder, 'Did he believe bearing the banner of the weak, the downtrodden, prosecuted ones, could make any difference – or perhaps a great difference?' I continue to ponder this thought, and the more I learn about the master of this home, the closer I feel to him. Again, I tell you, dear reader, history reminds us that he, too, was a survivor, suffering under heavy blows. For deeds of non-compliance, he carried the burden of professional, financial and family ruination, ignoring a dictator's decree. It was similar to my mother's predicament, as she, too, bore her own heavy blows of potential impending doom. Both survived living with unrelenting scars until the end. I, a descendant, am forever indebted and truly recognize and feel a deep special love for Aristides de Sousa Mendes. I say with certainty, it is plain to understand, without his existence as a compassionate human being, I would not exist, nor my descendants. For him, there will always be reverence within me.

With each footstep I take, I believe the noble dwelling perched high atop a hill, visible from miles around, stood as a symbolic beacon of humanity. Townspeople living within the surrounding countryside, still to this day, tell wonderful stories of the diplomat while photographers capture history of the present day Sousa Mendes family recalling its time of glory as well as its time of demise. The noble residence over the years is a reflection of family history. It is no wonder his descendants work strenuously toward restoring his honor acknowledging devotion to those in need.

The restored exterior of Casa do Passal,
Aristides' home.

Honored in Israel, a tree was planted in his name within the Martyrs' Forest near Jerusalem. And in 1988, Portugal posthumously rewarded him and returned to him diplomatic status, promoting Aristides to the position of Ambassador.

Still wandering about the first floor level, a private moment of thought captures my attention. I envision Aristides sitting alone, absorbed in world events. His lap crowded with papers received daily, details of war events received by diplomatic dispatches and cablegrams. How does he make sense of it? I envision him pondering these turbulent events occurring during the late 30s. Perhaps beliefs about the ensuing European crisis began to crystallize in this very house. Here, he may have fervently considered what to do. Perhaps a decision – a decision for action – action for righteous deeds steeped in humanity. But what will be the outcome and what will be the consequences, considering all possibilities. Pondering everything, it most probably, in my opinion, comforted his devout humanitarian heart – and the rest is history.

With such thoughts filling my mind, I marvel at my ability to maintain composure and avoid a flood of tears from pouring across my cheeks. Emotions easily drift to the surface after stepping foot in his home and on the surrounding grounds. In the near distance is the family's private chapel. I step outside for a breath of air.

After wandering about for a short period of time, Olivia calls us to attention. Mariana Abrantes, a board member and Mendes historian, wants to tell us something important. A question received from The Foundation needs the descendants' opinion. An immediate thought rings clear in my mind. *Anything the Foundation needs, I'm with them.* I feel so much a part of everything. My heart thumps, the emotion of joy rises and I'm mentally invested, determined to help provide input. I surmise it has something to do with completion of the renovation.

Then the question is posed: Should the interior of the home become a house-museum complete with decor of the day: wall coverings, furniture, re-furnished kitchen and a study as well as the third floor dormitory? Or, should it be developed as a museum portraying history of the Iberian peninsula, including persecutions and expulsions over hundreds of years?

This important question could not be answered with an immediate response. Therefore, the group, by now quite cohesive, would soon spent many breakfasts and lunches discussing merits of both alternatives. Regarding funding the project, financial sums had been donated by the Portuguese Government primarily channeled through private donations. In addition, the Sousa Mendes Board of Directors, lead by Olivia Mattis, thanked many in our group because of their involvement in fundraising. Substantial sums had been provided by descendants. Many functioned as diplomats, prominent businessmen and women, and second and third generation professionals, including authors, actors, attorneys, and respected philanthropists. All five Steppel descendants would contribute to this cause at the "Freedom Gala" held later that year in New York City.

The still unrestored interior foyer of Casa do Passal.

We end our day in Cabanas de Viriato visiting the family-owned church, an impressive building. Exiting the home, we walked a short distance to the estate's family cemetery where Aristides and wife, Angelina, are interned within a family mausoleum. Although the cemetery is not very large, 99 percent, if not all, grave headstones were comprised of gleaming white stone creating an eerie feeling – a virtual sea of white.

After concluding remarks from family members and before our bus meets us, Olivia suggests we say Kaddish. I take up the opportunity to complete our morning and lead the Kaddish prayer in front of Jews and Gentiles alike.

This scene will stay with me forever etched in vivid detail. Fellow journeyers stand quietly under blue skies dotted with puffy white clouds listening to my heartfelt recitation.

The visit and Kaddish prayer at the mausoleum of Aristides and Angelina was for me a difficult and emotional undertaking. Kaddish is a hymn whose origins, meaning and customs are, to me, familiar. Neither death, nor the deceased, are mentioned during the prayer recited in the Aramaic language, an ancient form of Hebrew, extolling G-d's virtues. It's considered a participatory prayer involving a congregation, or minyan, including the chanting of Amen in agreement. Although knowing that Aristides and his wife were devout Catholics, tradition holds that within Judaism it's not customary to recite Kaddish for non-Jews. But in this very special case, it was most appropriate to praise G-d knowing Aristides and Angelina were intensely religious people. In my heart and in my mind, it is fitting for them.

Words cannot express how heartwarming the final few minutes are at the Sousa Mendes cemetery. They are concluded at a very personal level. Looking into the faces of descendants, Foundation board members and everyone else engaged within this momentous journey, I can see that all are affected.

This creates an indelible, emotionally charged impression to last a lifetime.

The Sousa
Mendes
Cemetery

I look up at blue skies, envisioning my mother's face formed within one puffy white cloud. From heaven, I believe, she smiled down at me and was very proud.

From the cemetery, we travel to Sousa Mendes Middle School. Although already the end of June, students are on summer break, yet nearly 75 percent, and most of the faculty, returned to honor us with a musical program and slideshow followed by a reception. There is no doubt students and faculty highly regard Sousa Mendes as a hero, and by meeting descendants of visa recipients, this is considered a meaningful, exciting event. In addition, Dr. Lissy Jarvik, one of the surviving visa recipients, her fame known to the students, draws considerable excitement with her presence. Swarming around her, they touch and engage her with questions. Lissy's grown granddaughters stand close, watching as she humbly holds court.

Lissy Jarvik answers questions posed to her by students.

We are also told the school grounds are imbued with history, where there often are outdoor displays depicting historical events of Aristides as well as Holocaust remembrances. We regard student presentations as impressive and emotional.

A final event in honor of our visit engages us in an art project.

Members are presented with two-inch by two-inch square ceramic tiles to be adorned any way we want before being kiln fired, then affixed within an outdoor mall.

My ceramic tile is etched with my mother's name, birth date, date of passing, a Star of David and the endearing words, "Emah- Mother--Saved by Sousa Mendes." With heartfelt thanks for everything shown and given to us, we drive away, emotionally drained and exceedingly happy.

The City Of Porto, Portugal

June 30, 2017

Porto is Portugal's second largest city after Lisbon. Walking about this scenic city, we see narrow, very hilly streets all leading down to the river. This region of Portugal, encompassing Porto, is famed for growing grapes and production of Port. It's no secret to any wine lover that the primary allure of Porto is, quite simply, its port wine. "Touting a history that birthed the world's first demarcated wine appellation in the mid-18th century – long before Bordeaux was first classified in 1855, the Porto region has earned a permanent spot on the list of top worldwide wine destinations." (*Fodor Travel-October 29, 2013*).

Enormous vaulted cellars stretch along the banks of Porto's Douro River. Within these cellars, crafting port wine is a tradition stretching back hundreds of years. In addition, this beautiful hillside city today is noted for its mazes of cobblestone streets, sun-baked red-roofed buildings and a beautiful riverfront. Winding along the riverfront are houses hundreds of years old. Bright pink and blue exteriors reflect sunlight, causing a glistening effect. Directly below these homes, the riverfront is lined, one after the other, with cheerful cafes and restaurants beckoning strolling young people and tourists from around the world. These delightful havens offer culinary delights while others offer a simpler fare of coffee and fancy desserts. Their artful appearance beckons passersby to "Come – enjoy the river view with a glass of fine port wine and tempting desserts."

The current day Porto train station

The beautiful tile work at the train station as it was in 1940.

Our guides gather the group together and inform us that we have several leisurely hours free to enjoy soaking up local culture along riverside attractions.

We amble into a beautiful café, the Majestic. Walking toward its inviting open veranda, Sandy and I seat ourselves at a table beneath a colorful canopy. A waiter welcomes us with a smile and hands us menus. A brief summary written on the menu highlights the café's history dating back to 1921. Often, it was frequented by notable writers and philosophers, as well as other intellectuals of the day. Reading further, the written description mentions successful present-day author, JK Rowling, who frequented this establishment while writing her *Harry Potter* books.

Thoughts shift to my mother. Could she have found a few moments to sit here, as we do now, enjoying a cup of coffee – perhaps alone, or with new acquaintances?

Looking up, and in the near distance, I see a railroad station a short walk from the café. Its location is very convenient, I say to myself, for refugees, including my mother. Traveling by rail transport between cities was necessary to attain documents for their journey of escape.

We place our order, then gaze at the beautiful scene before us. Again, I'm quiet, reflecting upon my mother's ever-present journey for survival. Was she now more relaxed in Portugal having outrun Nazi pursuers? I try to assure myself. Leah, the family organizer, must have sighed a sense of relief. But then my thoughts turn in a radically different direction. I sense fear-filled stress overwhelming her mind, knowing she must find a way to procure visas for each family member. She must travel back and forth between Portuguese cities, pursuing government officials with renewed intensity to grant documents for emigration.

December 8, 1940

"Today is my 20th birthday – 'a beautiful age' someone told me yesterday (whom I told about it). Looking back over the past year I have to remark that I never had such a colorful and changing year! How many disappointments, how many destroyed hopes! But, if I take the  *accounting, everything is bad. Who knows where we will be next year on my birthday. Maybe under better conditions. That is my birthday wish!*

These are my thoughts on my birthday:

Other people are happy on their birthday getting presents and celebrating the day in the circle of their friends and acquaintances. They do not reflect for a moment on what has happened before or what will occur in the future."

Diary entries reveal that sums of money were needed for this purpose. Fortitude to persevere pushed her forward under an "umbrella" of charm, guile and cordiality with her piercing blue eyes and a crown of blonde hair. No doubt, I say to myself, she's a persistent young woman. I wonder on, marveling, "How does this youthful woman continue her quest, her mission of survival for self and family?" These, and many more questions course through my mind. And who will provide answers to these mysteries? Grudgingly, I know there are no answers. Only shrouded truths exist, and this I must accept.

Our waiter returns, balancing two clinking, red-hued

wine glasses, and sets them upon our small table. I raise my glass and focus on Sandy's face and smile at him with a clear message: Let's enjoy this day, this place, and each other. An hour slowly drifts by. I am more relaxed.

Portuguese currency is left on the table and we walk toward Porto's old Jewish quarter, visiting the Kadoorie Synagogue, known best by its official name: Mekor Chaim.

Built around 1900, the Synagogue functions as the center of Jewish life. Inside its darkened interior, it's easy to envision my mother and her family in 1940, passing though Porto, able to participate in a Shabbat service, joining with the Portuguese congregation.

Now in 2017, we observe the temple's president standing on an impressive bimah, a raised platform, in front of the synagogue's great hall. He tells our group about the 1506 expulsion of Jewish citizens residing in this city. Fortunately, many years later, a new synagogue was constructed. Continuing, he describes what occurred in 1940.

After being processed for exit visas in the city of Vilar Formoso, the Porto Jewish community played an important part helping refugees from all over Europe by providing safe haven along their path of escape – including my family.

Sabbath eve descends at the end of this pleasant day, and members of our group are invited to a Friday night Sabbath dinner joining prominent Jews of Porto. Unfortunately, only a small number remain. But there is hope the Jewish population will increase and thrive due to relocation of Sephardic Jews now leaving France. A wonderful day and evening of visiting historic Porto is firmly planted in my memory.

Mekor Chaim,
fully restored
and functioning.

Standing at the
Douro River,
Porto

Curia, Portugal - Then and Now

July 1, 2017

After a full day in Porto, we depart for Curia, a small hamlet northeast of Porto. I recall being told that during a previous journey, led by the Mendes Foundation, of which I was not yet a member, the Palace Hotel had not been included in the itinerary. I believe during this year's historic visit, the hotel was included due to my presence and that of Mark Ginsberg, both our parents having spent time there during crisis years.

Olivia thoroughly researched my mother's journey, having read her diaries. She graciously presents me with a gift, that this year's itinerary would include a stop at Curia (Koo-ree-a), and the Grand Palace Hotel. My desire to do so is motivated by a long-hidden photo album I had no access to until after my mother's final departure in 1982. Although I knew the album existed I did not know its contents. Finally, I decided to closely examine it. Lifting open the cover, I saw photos of a young women twenty years of age – my mother, Leah. But I had no knowledge of any of the other people also pictured. Leah obviously knew them and identified each with hand-written descriptions. The album's cover was titled "Monticello." The mystery unfolds. Its title revealed, it had been created after my mother had been living in the United States, most likely vacationing in Monticello, a resort town north of New York City. The album itself presented a poignant situation, and yes, another mystery. Old photos, a bit faded, mostly two-inch by two-inch pictures in black and white, border edges jagged. Images of people and places I know nothing about, people immortalized within the camera's eye. This album was never shown or discussed with my mother. These photos captured a time prior to Leah's final escape from Europe.

Drawn into the photo scenes, I am fascinated. My eyes focus on one image of young Leah elegantly dressed in a stylish suit coordinated with a fabulously chic broad brimmed hat worn to a jaunty angular tilt. The photo presents a striking portrait of her strolling down a street in Antwerp, Belgium. She carried a clutch bag in hand – so very glamorous, I must admit, presenting herself perhaps as a young enterprising woman. What was she doing in Antwerp that day? Who was the photographer – a passerby, a girlfriend, a gentleman friend, a family member? Why did she take time to pose for photos? Was she going someplace special, a consulate, perhaps, meeting an influential person who may offer supportive help during a time of crisis?

I know from her accounts that she needed others to help her and the entire Steppel family escape. I've read articles about farsighted, realistic Jewish citizens of Germany who were aware escape was their only chance. Many questions percolate within my mind about these photos, but for now, there are no answers, and probably never will be within my lifetime. But, there was a silver lining connected to the mysterious album. I didn't realize until I became associated with the Sousa Mendes Foundation, that many of these preserved photos harbor clues about the path my mother followed to freedom.

Arriving in Curia, Portugal, we now enter the world of the Grand Palace Hotel. I'm anxious to connect photos from the mysterious "Monticello" album with actual locations we now stand upon. Exiting the bus, Sandy bounds with the enthusiasm of an explorer. The landscaped grounds open a vista before us, presenting a magnificent view replete with gardens, a pond with a resident swan, and in the distance, the Grande Palace Hotel. It is an enormous hotel, one of the last remaining hotels of the Belle Epoch era, with its heyday during the first few decades of the twentieth century. I also learn that the hotel is located in the center of Portugal's wine region. This area is also renowned for medicinal retreats, thereby gaining the name Curia, with the meaning "water that cures." Fresh water springs, more than a thousand years old, provide its curative nature.

Hotel grounds boast a casino surrounded by beautiful parks – this, too, Leah describes in her diaries. These elegant features have been restored in the spirit of its original glory during grandeur years until the outside world was plunged into the chaos of war. We separate from the group and Sandy immediately starts clicking away, taking photos in exact spots that are depicted in photos from 1940 in my mother's album. Sandy is an exacting photographer and positions me in different settings he's memorized from my mother's photos. His goal is to duplicate the old black and whites with me in the exact places where my mother was photographed. I follow the photographer's directions and as I do, more and more, again and again, I walk in my mother's footsteps.

Passing a large pond replete with a floating swan, we arrive at the hotel's front doors. In front of these doors are chairs, and Sandy directs me, composing the photo shoot. Checking to make sure I'm positioned in the right spot, he pulls out one of Leah's black and whites, checking it against how I should be sitting. In the old black and white, Leah sits in front of a carved iron railing wearing a beautiful hat. I'm directed as to where and how to sit and position myself –

the camera clicks. I'm frozen in time and space. Captured in time like my mother, breathing life from old photos into the present. It warms my heart to re-create scenes seventy-plus years later in the exact positions in which she was photographed, circa, 1940. Overwhelmed by the re-enactment, I quell inside with joy. It is surreal, to say the least. Again, one more fantastically memorable experience draws me ever closer to my mother and her footsteps. There is a power in this mother–daughter connection, both of us within the same locations.

After all photo shoots are completed, Sandy and I enter the hotel. The interior has been restored to exactly as it had been during its refined years, decades earlier. The main lobby pays homage to its origins, preserving the original elevator surrounded by long forgotten luggage reverting back to the 1920s and '30s era.

After lunch, Mark Ginsberg, a fellow journeyer, speaks of his mother, Ina, who was also in Curia, most likely at the same time as Leah. Mark's mother's story was also fraught with intrigue and near disaster because, even though there was passage out from Portugal, she was not allowed to disembark in Mexico, New York City, or Norfolk, Virginia, and would have been forced to return to Europe. Somehow a miracle was at hand as she was able to contact lawyers in New York who intervened on her behalf by cabling Eleanor Roosevelt, wife of President Franklin D. Roosevelt. This magnificent woman traveled to Norfolk accompanied by immigration officials, and permitted Mark Ginsberg's mother and other shipboard refugees to enter the United States. Later in life, I was informed, Ina became a social doyenne, a woman who is the most respected in a particular field – a fashion muse and friend to the talented Andy Warhol. In addition, Ina became a cultural icon, a celebrated arts patron and helped found the Washington National Opera.

Considering the world around her, I believe Leah was indeed fortunate at being able to reside in Curia's Grand Palace Hotel, even though it was only for a four-month interlude, enjoying beauty, comfort, and peace. Walking these grounds warms my heart, knowing that within the cauldron of German armies overrunning Europe, my mother experienced a modicum of peace and elegant living.

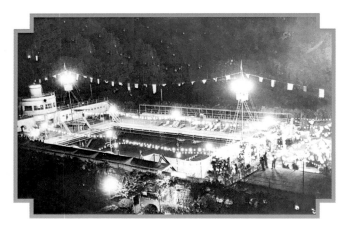

The Palace Hotel has saved historical photos. This is one of the pool area marked "Night Festival."

Leah at the outdoor bar of the Palace Hotel.

Rebecca at the same outdoor bar.

Above: Leah, far left, wearing a hat, at the lake park with friends; *Below:* The lake park today.

Above: Leah and friends in a row boat at the lake; *Right*: Today, a red rowboat is parked along the same shore.

Above and below:
Mother and daughter at the same exact spot in
front of the Palace – 78 years apart.

Left: Leah and a friend atop the water tower at the Palace's
pool; *Right:* Rebecca in 2017 at the same tower,
which has been well-preserved.

Leah, far left, made fast friends
with an Indian commissioner and his son, an Englishman,
and a journalist, at The Palace Hotel, August, 1940.

Above: Rebecca stands at the main doors
to the Palace Hotel;
Below: Leah, a passenger in a very elegant car,
partially hidden by the windshield, at the very same entrance!

A view from the Palace Hotel's magnificent gardens.

Foundation travelers make several stops, including Figueira da Foz, Portugal, where Lissy Jarvik lived in 1940, a place of sun and sea. A city at the mouth of the Mondego River, with extensive beaches of soft white sand, Figueira da Foz invites visitors and citizens alike for a relaxing holiday with its uniqueness of being a real fishing port mixed with cosmopolitanism. Here, we spend a day that includes a visit to the small row home where Dr. Lissy Jarvik resided as a young girl.

Our group leaves Figueira da Foz on the evening of July 2, arriving at Hotel Dom Pedro Palace, Lisbon, in time to settle in and meet for dinner. My anticipation heightens as we've been told there's a big surprise in store for the travelers.

February 5, 1941

"So, as my father would say, we risked it. We had gone to the American Consul. All our anxieties were relieved. We were well received and no tricky questions were asked of us. I assume that we made a good impression. Unfortunately, we only presented with a small sum of money. We were asked  to return in fourteen days; eight have already gone by. Once again we pray for good luck that we will be received well and be successful. That is the American business.

Regarding my lessons, which had been going steadily upwards, now it rapidly declines. One cannot count on the Portuguese. In the beginning they were all enthusiastic; the one who was the most ardent gave it up. Surely, the others will follow.

Na, we hope to leave soon anyway, and I won't regret anything here. Meanwhile, I hope to shop cheaply. If possible, directly from the manufacturer. I have already ordered a blouse. I found a pair of shoes, which I bought 'direct' and they were quite cheap and a great value. I never thought I'd find a pair of shoes to fit. This shopping spree I like."

Portugal
Exodus From Lisbon

July 2-3, 2017

Our travels are fast coming to a close with the next stop, Lisbon, the end point before fleeing refugees departed Western Europe heading in all directions. Lisbon is the capital and largest city of Portugal and is continental Europe's westernmost capital city, the only capital along the Atlantic coast. Lisbon is recognized as a global city because of its importance in finance, commerce, media, entertainment, arts, international trade, education and tourism.

Once within metropolitan Lisbon, it's important to the group to visit the Shaare Tikvah Synagogue, where Jewish refugees had gathered during 1940. Based on historical records, we are informed, Rabbi Menachem Mendel Schneerson visited this Lisbon synagogue accompanied by his wife, Chaya. Rabbi Schneerson was known as the Rebbe of the Lubavitcher Hasidic dynasty and is considered one of the most influential Jewish leaders of the 20th century. He and his wife eventually boarded the Portuguese liner, Sherpa Pinto, arriving safely in New York marking a revival of Judaism for old world refugees.

Leah and her parents could have very well listened to a sermon by this renowned Jewish scholar. Thinking about the information relayed to us, I wondered, did Rabbi Schneerson receive a visa from Sousa Mendes?

More uncovered research, and more startling findings. We visit the Portuguese Foreign Ministry archives finding evidence of a visa issued to Salvador Dali, a Spanish artist

101

perhaps best known for his painting of melting clocks titled, "The Persistence of Memory." Unfortunately, the rise of fascist leader Francisco Franco in Spain led to the artist's expulsion from the Surrealist movement. But that didn't stop him from painting, having received a visa from Sousa Mendes that allowed him and his Russian born wife, Gala Diakonova, to travel from Portugal to New York. During World War II and several years after, they remained in the United States until 1948 when both moved back to his beloved Catalonia, Spain.

While in Portugal, Leah writes in her diary about her frustration procuring funds needed to purchase tickets to transport the family away from Europe. Sufficient funds were needed for this purpose, and in order to attain the money, she needed to rely on help from other Jewish refugees waiting in Lisbon. Cooperation was often difficult among the thousands awaiting departure – not always patiently. Eventually, mutual assistance was found and Leah writes about friends "pooling resources," but beyond the mention of "pooling" available funds, no further details were written into her diary.

I think about my mother's struggles to accomplish her mission to obtain passenger ship tickets. She felt a sense of safety and comfort having entered Portugal, leaving capture and worse, behind, yet I feel pangs of anxiety for her predicament. Somehow, in Lisbon, I virtually sense my mother's constant state of stress – a plaguing tension. Looking into the heart of this beautiful Portuguese city, I'm thrust back in time, visualizing a persistent young woman kept awake with dreadful thoughts over sleepless nights, attempting to devise ways to obtain final visas and five tickets. Not until she is safely steaming toward a safe haven country with the entire family will she truly know she's escaped her pursuers. My questions continue: Did she have help? Were her parents involved at all in the long complex process of escape? Did she devise a method to obtain needed documents and ... did she keep records of her attempts? How many years could she survive, maintaining readiness to run from one place to another, one city to another, with only a moment's notice? This cloud of darkness must have hung low and heavy over her head. My thoughts fraught with worry continue. It's difficult churning up dark thoughts. But I have no doubts as I walk further along in my mother's journey. I come up for air and make an effort to clear my mind, desiring to return to the present, to the group, and most of all, to Sandy.

We stroll along extensive areas of the port. I am quiet, immersed again in my thoughts, walking a mile or two along busy port facilities. Sandy knows what I'm thinking. He does not try to make small talk, he is patient and I thank him with a smile – my hand held firmly in his.

My memory reaches back to information I discovered, stipulating Leah had a visa dating back to 1927, when the family lived in Poland, then moved to Düsseldorf, Germany. Another visa I uncovered in my parents' home had a stamp marked "Port au Prince, Haiti." This, I'm sure, was the family's "Plan B" – escape to anywhere sailing away from Lisbon. Thinking about the island nation of Haiti as a destination, and how she received a visa, is a mystery in and of itself. Some refugees had passage visas heading to diverse cities, including Havana, Philadelphia, Rio de Janeiro, and New York. Well-to-do refugees, I learned, were able to book passage and afford expensive seats aboard Clippers, the "flying ships" of Pan Am, linking America to Europe on twice-per-week flights. When the 1930s drew to a close,

Pan Am secured and maintained vital air routes in a world increasingly fraught with danger. Flying ships were able to provide service to any city with a sheltered harbor, making them the ideal international airliner at a time when few cities had runways capable of handling large land planes. But, for the majority of refugees able to make their way to Lisbon, Portugal, they had but one option: obtain necessary visas and secure passage aboard a Portuguese liner crossing the Atlantic.

Although life was calmer upon reaching Portugal than it had been during the past two years on the run, the Steppel family's objective was clear – leave Europe any way they could. With this important driving force consuming the family in 1940 Lisbon, it brings to mind the famous French writer and future fighter pilot, Antoine de Saint-Exupery. He wrote, "The very idea of happiness was staged so that G d could believe it still existed." Among everything else, the Steppel family held this idea in high regard.

We continue to walk beside concrete and wood piers jutting out like blunted fingers into dark blue Atlantic waters. Frenetic energy of dock workers mix within a cacophony of noise filling the air. But the outside world becomes muted as my mind again swirls with questions.

Did the family have a time frame by which they hoped or needed to leave? Had they run out of money? Was her younger sister, Henni, and brother Paul, in Lisbon, or had they remained in Curia while the now twenty-one-year-old family leader banged on embassy doors and continuously made the rounds of piers and shipyards trying to find passage?

I wondered, "How did Leah procure sufficient funds to purchase five tickets? How many ships did she approach? Was there a central transportation office with thousands waiting for an open ticket? On and on, question after question, fills my mind and I wish I could somehow put them all to rest.

Yet, hope still lived, I learned. Desperately frantic refugees visited understaffed consulates, crowded travel agencies, waited long hours in queues hoping to obtain financial and administrative assistance provided by relief organizations. And Leah, I know, was in the middle of the chaos, the stress, the fear, yet she held hope combined with belief in the Almighty and her lucky star. I know this from diary entries I've memorized, carried deep within me, now a part of me.

February 19, 1941
Portugal

"Yesterday we were at the American Consulate to try our luck. I believe that our fortune does not lie in America, since it is impossible for us to get there. The Consul denied our visa application. I asked the Secretary to get permission from the Consul to let me speak to him  *personally. This was also denied. Thereupon, I spoke to the vice-consul, since I was used at the consulate as an interpreter. He did, in fact, talk to the Consul himself about our case. This turned out to be of no use either. Now, we must obtain a new affidavit, or America is OVER ."*

Diary entries reveal a sense of desperation in trying to work with HICEM, one of the Hebrew relief organizations. Leah writes about a handful of aide societies and how grateful she is for their existence.

I'm amazed at the momentous moving picture clearly rolling across my mind, of Leah always pushing her mission forward. I feel her pain within my own body, my soul clearly recognizing her anxious thoughts. She had successfully escaped the German net, trudged across great swatches of Western Europe, survived numerous aerial bombardments, police patrols, border guards and hid on traveling trains for weeks on end. Always, wherever she was before reaching Portugal, she slept with one eye open guarding survival. For me, it's almost incomprehensible!

A thought crosses my mind. What if she was unable to attain the issuance of a third visa from the American Consul, thereby providing documents for each of the five Steppels? But once all visa were obtained, I assured myself within my thoughts, she could begin the quest for the family's ocean passage.

Left: The final stamped exit visa allowing Leah's departure from Lisbon bound for New York! *Below:* The final visa photos taken for their passage on the Nyassa, (approximately April 13, 1941)

PINCUS STEPPEL

HANNA GUSTA STEPPEL

ITTA STEPPEL NÉE LAUS

HORSZCZ STEPPEL

OLIVIA LEA STEPPEL

March 11, 1941

The Steppels, through persistence, faith, and good luck, receive final visas! And, with this achievement, Leah's faith in G-d grows more intense during the following days. Booking passage on a ship is now her main focus. Her diary states she stayed at a hotel in Lisbon with a friend. Yet, she remains in despair, searching for necessary funds to purchase ship passage.

July 3, 2017

In one of Olivia Mattis' emails sent before the journey began, she requested all members of the group bring at least one dressier outfit, including a sport jacket for men. At dinner on July 2, we're informed the office of Portugal's president had approved and arranged for a visit with

President Marcelo Rebelo Sousa, the sitting president. Wow! Portuguese presidents wield significant influence and authority, especially in the fields of national security and foreign policy. Our entire group was agog with anticipation. We had passed the Palace entrance the day before and had seen smartly uniformed guards at the gate.

Our tour bus makes its way up a small hill leading to our destination. From afar, we can see the building itself designed in several sections, each painted a lively pink with white trim. We're met by the presidential photographer, a journalist, and several of the president's assistants. Our group is accompanied by Dr. Olivia Mattis, Aristides' grandson, Gerald, and Aristides' nephew, the son of Aristides' twin brother, Cesar. We are led upstairs to an enormous, beautifully appointed, ante room. Our eyes widen with amazement as we notice magnificently upholstered sofas and chairs, large murals and other artwork displayed around the room. We roam about, take photos, and enjoy the view overlooking formal gardens. Our voices are hushed as we marvel at impressive sights before our eyes.

Shortly, an assistant enters, requesting us to proceed toward a large veranda. We do so. Within moments, the president, a tall, distinguished looking gentleman, enters through a side door, shaking hands as he engages one after another visitor with warm, softly spoken words. The tall gracious gentleman walks toward me as I stand with another group member, a woman with my mother's first name, Leah Sills. I learn both her father and grandfather were issued visas by Sousa Mendes. Ms. Sills had recently joined our group for this very special occasion. She and I both realize we have a common feature – azure blue eye color with a dark navy rim. This feature is most unusual, so much so that I've never come in contact with anyone else having it – until now! Within a minute's inquiry, we ascertain both her father and my mother were born in the same Polish city of Lodz. Are we somehow related? Overhearing our brief conversation, President Marcelo Sousa turns toward us, also recognizing our strikingly similar eye color. He smiles at both of us and I move closer, thanking him for agreeing to this most generous meeting and for his country being openly receptive to my mother, and thousands of others seventy plus years ago.

The 2017 Journey to Freedom travelers
with Marcelo Rebelo Sousa, President of Portugal,
at the Presidential Palace in Lisbon

Taking my gracious remarks to heart, he plants a warm kiss on my cheek. With his gesture firmly planted in my heart, he invites the group to be embraced, recognized and remembered in a photo. We follow him down a flight of stairs toward the gardens. With brisk strides, he leads and I walk right in step with him providing a few brief moments to converse while others follow behind. He shares with me how important Aristides' actions were and how his government is supportive toward popularizing his memory by any means possible. I am transfixed, as though I am my mother, thanking the president personally for Aristides de Sousa Mendes' heroism seventy years before.

Left: Rebecca strolls with Portuguese President Marcelo Rebelo Sousa, while thanking him for Aristides de Sousa Mendes' heroism.

Right: Rebecca and the President share a hug after their talk.

April 4, 1941

Leah has found a ship for passage! The Nyassa, a cargo ship sailing from the port of Lisbon. Passage for the family secured at last. Her diary entries suddenly stop after this notation.

Many years later, I find in the sanctuary of her red "secretary," a faded black and white newspaper clipping from *The New York Daily Mirror* portraying two beautiful sisters. The family's new life had begun in America.

Right: The Port of Lisbon, 2017.
Below: When I asked my mother how she came to the United States, her answer was, "On a banana boat."

May 15, 2018

Over the last six months I have been invited to share my mother's story and our journey.

One such presentation rewarded me when a man approached afterwards to tell me that he had information about the Nyassa. His longtime friend, Elfriede Morgenstern, now deceased, was born in Frankfurt in 1927. Her father, who came to America, was unable to get his family out until the opportunity to board the Nyassa, certainly on the same sailing as the Steppels. Peter sent me both a manifest, and more importantly, an article from *The New York Times*, written on April 27, 1941! This paralleled the photo of my mother and Henni in *The New York Daily Mirror*, dated April 26.

The Times' byline reads: "Tiny Liner brings 816 from Europe." The report stated that the ship was reminiscent of the "old steerage days" and ported in Brooklyn, New York. On Nyassa's previous trip in December, 1940, it held 451 passengers and was filled to capacity. Now the ship arrived with 816 passengers, with double deck beds set up for the refugees where merchandise usually was stored. It continues stating that the ventilation was very poor and there was almost no room to move. There was one lavatory for 200 people and the sanitary conditions were deplorable. My heart just breaks as I read the news article. There were even reports that passengers were defrauded in Portugal by "speculators" who took bonuses before passage on the ship could be obtained. The cost ranged between $160 for third class (in the cargo holds) to $480 for first class. Where were the Steppels? Did Leah procure enough money for first class? Were the Steppels part of the complaining passengers? Did their health suffer?

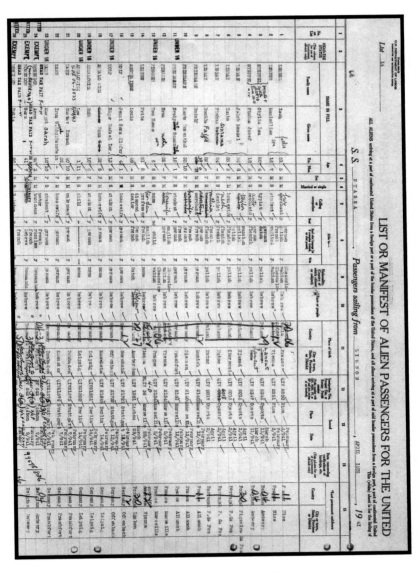

A rare find, the manifest from the Nyassa.
Otylia and Pincus are the 3rd and 4th on the list.

113

(Mirror)

Otylia Lea Steppel (left), 20, and sister, Henny, 15, refugees from Poland. They lived in French train for 10 weeks.

Daily Mirror, dated April 26. We now know for certain the year is 1941. Caption reads: "Otylia Lea Steppel (left), 20, and sister Henni, refugees from Poland. They hid on a French train for 10 weeks."

Concluding Thoughts

March 1, 2018

More than thirty-four years have passed since I first leafed through the small hard cover bound diaries my mother left behind as a legacy – a legacy wrapped in mystery. And more than seventy-seven years have passed since Leah's thoughts, details, unknown names, and addresses were first inscribed upon diary pages. Through ensuing years since my mother's untimely passing, I could not come to grips with what lay between her diary pages -- my own life consumed with family responsibilities needing to come first in the role of a young mother. Though reflecting back, I now realize that fear within me caused procrastination. It was fear of unknown revelations laying dormant, untouched within the darkness of an unopened end table drawer.

Fourteen precious years sped by, my eyes never wanting to translate and know what existed within my mother's words, my mother's world. Always there existed a nagging impulse in back of my mind to find strength and to resurrect secrets penned by Leah's artistic German handwriting during a time when a twenty-year-old woman's life should have been spent in happy carefree days. Eventually, I had strength enough to read between diary covers, which made it abundantly clear that "carefree" was not her life during the desperate years of 1940-1941.

Through years of silence, I somehow knew a spark of motivation was needed for my fingers to finally open the diaries – and open my mind to learn about my mother's past. Finally, I found what I needed to begin this journey.

In 1996 when my son, Elliot, was turning thirteen, his Bar Mitzvah celebration culminated in a family trip to Israel. Yes, this is what I needed to motivate me, and I began delving into my mother's written accounts spanning two desperate years. Only then, I told myself, would I discover truths lying buried within.

My family celebratory motivational event set in motion a long struggle to translate her diary, which finally illuminated Leah's two-year journey in words and deeds. Within this seemingly interminable task, I began to truly learn about Otylia, Lena, and Leah Steppel.

Dr. Jacob Weiner became an important asset and friend throughout the translation process. Many questions took flight within my mind while we worked together, slowly lifting the fog of silence. His unrelenting efforts were a huge step forward. With Dr. Weiner's work concluded after months of careful translation, this task was followed by my research as I sifted through information from libraries and government agencies, focusing on the process of copyrighting both diaries. The next logical step after several months, with a copyright granted, was self-publishing translated diaries. And this, too, was accomplished.

Throughout the years, with all of my project's ups and downs, starts and stops, high and low times, my husband, Sandy, stood by me, helping with organizational details and never wavering from his positive attitude. He was the "wind beneath my wings," over many years walking with me down a twisting road of exploration, always at my side, standing fast, providing time for me to explore in my own way and with my own needs. To journey along a pathway that unraveled the mystery bound up with my mother and the mother-in-law, he too, truly loved.

Now that bright light of understanding shines upon my mother's penned words, the mother who gave birth and raised me, I recognize in her my own strength and life force – a reflection of my tenacity, perseverance, and curiosity. Her goodness runs through my veins, providing strength to face life's challenges in many ways similar to hers. Is this the end of my mother's unraveling legacy? No! Not by any means. More points of light are to be illuminated by my own blossoming memories of years spent with her, followed by knowledge of her poignant written words, describing what she accomplished under the heavy weight of life and death circumstances taking place seventy-seven years ago.

Delving deeper and reflecting more, I believe what I've penned within my memoir will help wash away silence between Otylia, Lena, Leah Steppel and me. Perhaps now, I think, in some ways, I'm closer to my mother than even during times when she was alive. I look to the heavens and believe there is more to be unearthed about Leah and about myself. Beyond the deep footsteps both of us walked in, a pathway had been found, lit with bright lights of truth and understanding to be passed on to descendants, sons, and grandsons, as well as unborn sons and daughters, helping them see more clearly their collective past and hopefully what the future brings.

Walking in my mother's 1940-1941 footsteps, I believe in my heart, we are interwoven with our journeys of 1940/'41 and 2017. The resurrection of a mother-daughter passage from Bordeaux, France to Lisbon, Portugal, was one of the most important times in my life. We, the descendants, are not born in isolation, even if our history was shrouded in silence. Lifting this silence makes us wiser and stronger people.

It is my hope and prayer that wherever my life's journey takes me, one of my descendants will lift the torch, passing the "fire" of memory and understanding ever onward, never extinguished into the distant future.

Mein Buch

My Diary
1939 - 1947

Otylia Lea Steppel

PART 2
THE DIARY — TRANSLATED

About the Translator

Three short months ago, Rabbi Jacob G. Wiener, Ph.D., was a stranger to me. Now, I consider myself blessed to have met such a fine gentleman, scholar, and patient soul.

Rabbi Wiener emigrated from Poland in 1938 where he was a teacher and liaison between the Jewish community and the Nazi authorities. His many years in New York were spent as Rabbi, teacher, accountant, social worker, and published writer.

Since his retirement, (which he explains as simply "putting on a new tire"), Rabbi Wiener moved to Silver Spring, Maryland, with Gertrude, his wife of forty eight years.

One has to look in any number of places to find the Rabbi. He is currently the Chaplain at two area nursing homes, JCC volunteer, and a docent at The United States Holocaust Museum.

When asked how I came to find the Rabbi, the answer is minor compared to: How is it that a stranger was convinced to undertake such a huge project? Once you have completed reading this compelling diary, the answer is clear.

My profound gratitude goes to Rabbi Wiener for seeing the importance of this diary and persevering under deadline pressures and my many questions.

1996

Foreword
(from 1996)

As we raced along the New Jersey Turnpike we knew it was too late. It was August 22, 1982, and we had been trying to get acquainted with our new daughter. We wanted to show her the ocean. Mom, as always, encouraged us to go on with life as "normal" while she once again returned to Mt. Sinai Hospital for treatment.

The new Dan Fogelberg song, "The Leader of the Band" gave us the sign:

" The leader of the band has died...
and (he) gave a gift to me I know I never can repay...
(he) earned his love through discipline..
(his) gentle means of sculpting took me years to understand...
(his) blood runs through my instrument...
and (his) blood runs through my soul...
My life has been a poor attempt to imitate the man...
I'm just a living legacy to the leader of the band..."

When we arrived in New York hours later Dad just looked at us with his sad mournful eyes. "She's gone."

Months later as I helped Dad go through Mom's things, I took the red felt folder, that she referred to as her "secretary" from her night table drawer. I knew it contained possessions and photos, but the details were never discussed when I was a child. Pieces of stories had surfaced over the years, but the diaries remained a mystery. When I returned home I simply placed them in my end table drawer.

Although I had her German written diaries translated onto audiotapes, I could not, at the time, bring myself to listen to them. I sent the originals to Mark and occasionally had the strength to look at the photos and papers.

When news was out that approval of a museum to document the Holocaust was impending, I set an appointment to meet the head curator. I will never forget walking through corridors of offices, seeing walls and walls of photos, and boxes of possessions. There were researchers working on documents, sifting through the only remains of a once proud European Jew.

The curator and I spent hours going through the diaries, passports, and documents.

"We are very interested in your mother's account. Currently the permanent displays for the future Holocaust museum has been determined, but we would put her possessions in our archives to be used for future exhibits."

If I agreed to give the diaries and documents to the museum they would be the property of the United States government.

"You can visit them anytime. Just call and make an appointment."

I was not ready to turn over this unknown legacy, so I returned home and put them back in the night table drawer. Almost a decade has passed, and now it is time. With the occasion of Elliot's Bar Mitzvah, and reading the book, "Putting G-d on the Guest List," I knew that the work would be well worth the discipline it would take to complete the task.

RYSOPIS — SIGNALEMENT

Żona — Femme

Rok urodzenia Date de naissance	*1892*
Miejsce urodzenia Lieu de naissance	*Łańcut pw. Łańc...*
Zatrudnienie Profession	*bez zajęcia* *sans profession*
Wzrost Taille	*średni* *moyenne*
Twarz Visage	*podłużna* *ałangé*
Włosy Cheveux	*ciemnoblond* *bland-foncé*
Oczy Yeux	*...* *brun*
Znaki szczególne Signes particuliers	*żadne* *nulles*

DZIECI — ENFANTS

Imię Nom	Wiek Age	P... S...
Stylja-Lea	*6 lat*	*...*
Pinkas-Józef	*4 "*	*...*
Hana-Gusta	*1 "*	*...*

Podpis urzęd...
Signature de l'age...

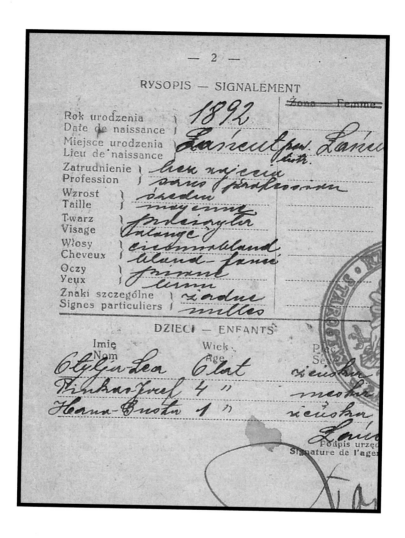

FOTOGRAFJE — PHOTOGRAPHIES

Podpis
Signature

Itta

Itta Steppel, my grandmother, is pictured on the family
Polish passport in 1927. My mother, Otylia-Lea, is on the
left, with her sister, Henni, and brother, Pincus Josef. They
are 6, 4, and 1 years old. Itta's birth date is documented
as 1892, four years older than my grandfather, Moses.
For more opportunities the family left Lancut, Poland, to
emigrate to Düsseldorf, Germany.

125

The Polish passport used by the Steppel family when they
emigrated from Lancut, Poland, to Düsseldorf, Germany.
Moses Steppel, male head of the family,
was issued a separate passport.

Gütermann & Co., Nähseiden=Fabriken, Gutach~Breisgau

18 January, 1939

Today, on January 18, 1939, I am beginning to write down all that happened in my life. It has been a life of many changes, never flowing very straight.

Now I am standing at the crossroads. I do not know what will lie ahead for me. Everything was going very evenly when we lived in Poland. My young years were rather monotonous. When I was seven years old I emigrated with my parents and siblings to Düsseldorf, in Germany.

Until the year 1933 everything went along smoothly and normally. My parents were working very hard and bitter to earn enough for their daily life. Then G-d[2] decided to punish us Jews by sending us a second Haman.[3] Thereupon our life was in constant fear and uneasiness regarding our future. No one knew what the next day would bring and there was also no possibility to run away from it.

„Union" = und „Compromiss" =Nähzutaten sind praktisch und billig!

---

1. Each diary entry is marked with these Hebrew letters which stand for "B'ezras Hashem": "With the help of G-d."

2. As was the custom, the name of The Almighty was never written out completely. Expressing His name fully was strictly meant for prayer and holy documents.

3. At nineteen, Leah's imagery and Jewish education drew her to aptly compare Hitler to the ancient evildoer, Haman.

I wrote to our relatives in America, in April of '38. We hesitated a long time, because we always hoped the situation here would change for the better. They sent us a positive reply and promised to do for us whatever they could.

Then the greatest calamity began: all Polish Jews had to leave Germany! In the evening, at exactly 12 o'clock midnight, in October of 1938, there was a knock on our door; the police were standing outside and requested entrance. They ordered my parents to immediately pack all their valuables [4] and come with them. With this they coldly declared that my parents would never again see their residence. My parents did not believe the officials, and went along, as they were, with empty hands. My brother was at the time in Frankfurt at the Yeshiva.[5] I, myself, was not home, but in the hospital.[6]

„Union" = und „ Compromiss" =Nähzutaten sind praktisch und billig !

---

4. History has proven the reason for telling Jews to pack valuables. This is the way the Nazis amassed fortunes from their Jewish victims.

5. A Jewish school combining religious and secular studies, often devoting a good portion of time to the study of the Talmud.

6. There is no mention as to the reason for Leah's hospitalization.

Only my little sister was at home, and she had to go along (with my parents).

At the police station they met many more Jews of the city. They had all come with bag and baggage. In short: all Jews were transported in cattle cars to Poland, except those who did not have their Polish passport. Luckily, my parents were among the latter. They were allowed to go home. Everything seemed to be in order again. They had spent a night and a day in prison.

The picture of Mojzesz (Moses) Steppel on the passport that he so fortuitously left at home. His date of birth is September 21, 1896. (Coincidentally, over a half century later, a granddaughter, Rebecca, is born on this same day.)

„Union" = und „Compromiss" =Nähzutaten sind praktisch und billig!

Approximately four weeks later, in November, (Crystal Night 9/10), the real excitement began. The October episode had Just been a prelude. A young Jewish boy, 17 years of age, shot and killed a German legate in Paris. Following this occurrence all the synagogues in German cities were set on fire in the middle of the night; all Jewish stores were plundered and smashed; show windows were nailed up with boards. It was the greatest scandal that people ever lived to see. With 20 to 25 men[7] they broke into private residences of the Jews, demolishing and destroyed everything breakable, even the people were not spared.

I myself saw on that day a girl with a totally disfigured face, completely battered and swollen. All of the German citizenship were led away and put in concentration or labor camps. The Poles saved themselves in the consulates. We also went there. Since there was only one room at our disposal, it got pretty filled up because people came from all the towns and surroundings. There was no place left to sit down. We were standing all the time; even the hallways were full of people.

„Union"= und „Compromiss"=Nähzutaten sind praktisch und billig!

---

7. History books record about 100.

February 25, 1939

I want to stop recalling the stories of old, even though I could tell you much more of misery and suffering, of broken lives, smashed limbs, and destroyed homes. But of that enough now. Let me start with a theme of hope, and how everything in the end turned out well and good.

One day, our dear Mother came home and asked us, "How would you like to go to Holland?" At that time, our whole thinking and striving was only towards emigration. At first we were very happy; nobody thought of the painful leave-taking and separation pain.

Thus it was decided that my little sister was to be the first one to go on December 8, 1938.[8] She was going all by herself into the unknown world. A friend of ours came with a motorcycle and took her to Heerland[9]. There she was to remain for eight days. I would follow her on the fifteenth of December. I, too, traveled by motorcycle and throughout the journey looked forward to seeing my sister, Henni, again. But, it was not meant to be.

„Union" = und „ Compromiss" =Nähzutaten sind praktisch und billig !

---

8. On Leah's birthday.

9. Holland

The day before (my arrival) she was sent to Amsterdam. Fourteen days later she was sent to a Home for Children in Hoogereen. She constantly wrote letters complaining about being homesick.
I cannot do anything to help her.

Young Henni Steppel

„Union" - und „Compromiss" -Nähzutaten sind praktisch und billig !

As I said (before), I came to Heerland and learned that my sister was no longer there. You can imagine my fright! Family G., where she spent her last days (before[10] continuing her travel), said that they were not allowed to lodge refugees. They sent me to Mr. H., who was the president of the aid committee. He was unavailable to talk to me at this hour. Someone telephoned a Mr. G. to come over, and he really came. He spoke to the man who brought me there (by motorcycle) and then he said, " Come along." He took me to his house, gave me something to eat and offered me a room. Since then I am here, which is now (already) ten weeks. In the meantime, he has helped me and my parents a lot. I expect (still) to talk about it...

The next morning, we had to go to the commissioner of the police to announce our presence and to register. The registration proceeded all right, but later I was summoned to the commissioner again.

---

10. December 15, 1938

This time he wanted to detain me and send me back![11]

With Mr. G.'s persistent intervention I was allowed[12] to return home, to the house of Mr. G. until Friday.

„Union" = und „Compromiss" = Nähzutaten sind praktisch und billig!

---

11. All Jews, especially refugees, were constantly filling out paperwork and official documents. These were required to keep track of Jews and their whereabouts. It is about this time that Leah took pen to hand and started "practicing" handwriting. She now also spoke at least three to four languages (German, Polish, Yiddish, French and possibly English as well).

12. Perhaps a bribe.

My request to remain had been submitted to Den Haag.[13] Again, Mr. G. did everything possible for me and he succeeded for me to stay in his house while I awaited the reply. The police are asking of my whereabouts. The commissioner calls the house to ask if there has been a reply. He tries again and again to keep me. I waited anxiously to know whether or not I would be able to stay.

After Henni and I had left, only my brother stayed behind (in Germany). He could not come because all Jews who left after us had all been returned. On January 1, 1939, his birthday, I learned from my parents that he arrived safely in Antwerp. After some not minor difficulties he succeeded entering a vocational school to be a mechanician. He also eventually found a room, (which is also hard to do here).

---

13. Capital of The Netherlands. It was the site for the high courts and decision making body of the government. Also known as The Hague.

But this room was not exactly clean and nice. Yet, he was in Antwerp – it was not easy, but he was out of harm's way. That was the most important.

Even if you suffer from hunger and frost, but you are no longer in the German Hell.

Now my parents are all alone (in Germany)! They have sent all their belongings away and were thinking to get away themselves.

February 28, 1939

On February 2nd, my dear mother departed trusting G-d would also help her, and this was good. She expected to be in Sittard (Holland) at three o'clock. So I traveled with Mr. G. to relatives in Sittard. I asked how to get to the border town, and got off at that place. It was misty all day. The highway was endless, no human in sight. I went onward looking for my mother.

After three-quarters of an hour I arrived at the barrier of the customs duty. The official let me pass when I showed him some letters. Between the two border posts of Germany and Holland I saw my mother. We were both very happy.

We went into a small restaurant nearby to talk all about our experiences. But I don't know anymore what we talked about. Then she gave me an address of the people who would bring her over.[14] I returned and she remained there.

This time I was stopped by soldiers who wanted to check my papers. I knew how to get free of them and went to the address given to me by Mother.

---

14. To Holland

Gütermann & Co., Nähseiden=Fabriken, Gutach~Breisgau

At first they did not want to help (bring my mother).

That drove me to despair! When I gave them the name of our relatives in Sittard, they were no longer disinclined. The young man went to my mother and told her to wait until evening. It was just four o'clock in the afternoon. I continued on to Sittard. Mr. G. had gone with his relatives to a funeral. When he returned home he immediately went with me to those people. Now they were willing, since they saw they could rely on prompt payment.

So we had to wait. We went to a cafe, ate some bread and butter with cheese, drank some coffee, and watched the clock.

To wait is terrible. Once the time had come, the people said they were going to pick up my mother. It was six thirty p.m. In one hour they would be back. Again we had to wait and wait. Our patience was greatly tested. The worst was, that by seven thirty they had still not arrived. Eight p.m. passed.

Shortly before nine p.m. they were back saying everything went well. They had crossed the border, but Mother was so tired she could not go any further.

The automobile that was to bring my mother to Antwerp had also been waiting for over an hour. The

„Union" = und „Compromiss" =Nähzutaten sind praktisch und billig!

138

chauffeur went to call for her, and we said good-bye. We went along with the car for a little bit. It was so foggy that one could not see his hand in front of it. It was hard for the driver to find his way. They did not continue traveling through the night, but stayed overnight (in a hotel). The next day they went on to Antwerp. It had been a terrible ordeal, as I was told later on.

I am happy, though, that my mother is finally here. She also comes just at the right time. My brother, Paul, was very sick in bed and there was nobody nursing him. She took care of him until he recovered. We thanked G-d that she came at the right time and that G-d spared him.

Brother Paul, in his
Air Force uniform.
He is perhaps 19
years old when this
photo was taken.

Everything appears to be easy and simple (to others) when you read this, but it was very difficult, and without Mr. G., who did very much for us, (rather, he did everything for us,) it would not have ended so well. Even our mother agreed that he (Mr. G.) had been a G-d send to us. I wanted to do something to show my gratitude to him. February 17th was his birthday. I had nothing to give him except congratulations. But Mrs. G., we gave a photo album and a shopping bag. They all liked the presents, and she herself was happy with it. This was only a small token of gratitude.

„Union" = und „Compromiss" =Nähzutaten sind praktisch und billig!

Gütermann & Co., Nähseiden=Fabriken, Gutach~Breisgau

*We cannot really ever repay what they, Mr. and Mrs.
G., actually did for all of us.*

This photo was found along with the diaries. Perhaps
this is the 'G' family Leah refers to so fondly.
The arrow points to Leah, in back.

„Union" = und „Compromiss" =Nähzutaten sind praktisch und billig!

February 28, 1939

Today I happen to have time and I want to devote it to trifling matters. Although today is housecleaning, but our girl [15] sent help, and I have, therefore, not much to do. So, first Mrs. G's birthday: already a few days before I was nervous. On that day the girl and I got up at five o'clock in the morning to be ready. We expected the visit of Mrs. G.'s sister.

---

15. We believe that Leah was a mother's helper, but the reference to "our girl" is unclear.

(short missing section of diary)

March 15, 1939
Heerlen/Holland

Today I want to talk about the great event. On March 4th, Pa crossed the border successfully! On the 10th he was with Mother in Antwerp. It went like this: at five p.m. the chauffeur came down and announced that he was going to Aachen (in Germany). He said he would be return(ing) in two or three hours. I awaited him around eight p.m. It was eight, it was nine; I was in a state of great excitation, as one might imagine. I went on a stroll with my little dog and when I came home again, the chauffeur had just been here. He had left a lexicon and fountain pen for me. He still had to bring my father. At about ten p.m. the telephone rings: my father from Aachen. He was in despair and was alone; the others had to leave. What should he do? I felt smashed. A telephone call to that particular driver gave no explanations for the delay.

I had to be strong and continue waiting. A dreadful word.

At ten thirty (o'clock) the bell rings. It was the lady of the house. She relates quite excitedly what happened. He (my father) was not let through. They had missed each other! They had waited one and a half hours at the designated place. In vain. She would go back to try a different approach.

Finally they arrived at half past twelve o'clock. They had hidden and continued to make attempts to get through.

Waiting seemed endless to me. My joy was boundless, especially since they had managed to escape from the (German) hell. The next day I learned that he had safely arrived in Antwerp. Everyone had been worried about him. All day I was mad[16] from joy. It had a contagious effect; everyone was glad. But this joy was to be short-lived.

---

16. A direct translation. We might write "delirious" with joy.

Mrs. G. was supposed to get up from her bed after an eight days' illness. She had been ill with the grippe. But she still felt weak, and got up the following day. It was an unsociable time for us all.

The woman of the house is the center of activity in a home. Everything hinges on her, especially here. It all seemed so still, since she was not downstairs (in the kitchen). Now she has recovered and things go on their normal course again.

March 19, 1939

Of my little sister I hear that, unfortunately, she is sick in bed. My mother says there is an outbreak of diphtheria amongst the children in Heerlen. I pray to G-d to protect her from that illness, and hope that in her situation it is only a minor cold. I cannot think of being sick and in a strange place. She has been absent from home for three months, but her home sickness increases daily. Perhaps my parents will succeed in moving her to Antwerp.

This would be a joy for Henni, although it would be another job for my parents; yet they would be happy to accept it. May G-d make it happen.

But first of all we wish her to be well. I hope she will be spared.

My parents have written to America that they have arrived in Antwerp. They received an immediate telegraphic message and twenty-five dollars by wire to help us along and make their life a little easier.

146

Gütermann & Co., Nähseiden-Fabriken, Gutach-Breisgau

They simply cannot join me until Henni is better. They are satisfied being together and they are waiting to see how G-d will guide them henceforth. With G-d's help it will all work out.

„Union"-und „Compromiss"-Nähzutaten sind praktisch und billig!

Gütermann & Co., Nähseiden-Fabriken, Gutach-Breisgau

March 29, 1939
Antwerp, Belgium

Man makes plans, but G-d directs.

On Sunday I was still in Heerlen. We played the game: "Man, don't ever get angry." We did not think of anything malicious to happen. On Monday, Mr. G. said, "At ten o'clock you have to go with me to the police" I was frightened and imagined the worst might happen. Family Goldstein[17] comforted me to the best of their ability. At ten we started out. It was as I thought. They wanted to bring me back over the border to Germany! Only due to the effort of Mr. G. I was not immediately kept there (at the police station) to be sent back. But I had to disappear. So I thought of Antwerp. The chauffeur was at once advised, and at two o'clock I said good-bye to my friends. It was very hard for us to leave, even the woman next door cried. But it was not parting forever.

„Union" - und „Compromiss" -Nähzutaten sind praktisch und billig !

---

17. This is the first mention of the name of her benefactors. This may have been an inadvertent slip, which may produce positive results. Perhaps someone will read this diary and come forward with information that leads to the Goldsteins and my sincere gratitude.

Gütermann & Co., Nähseiden=Fabriken, Gutach~Breisgau

After Pesach[18] they will visit me and we'll spend a good day. I am already looking forward toward it. I hope the weather will be fine.

The trip passed without any complications. I had a passport and visum.[19] Mr. G. accompanied me and on the way we bought food for my parents: butter, cheese, bread, coffee, vegetables, and chocolate.

Antwerp: My first impression was: why are so many Jews running around here? All businesses have Jewish signs. Up to now I have not seen much else but Jews (in Antwerp),

By special intervention we succeeded to notify (the police) immediately (of my arrival). I became acquainted with the Family Getzler, the people in whose store I worked, and I also discovered distant relatives. Luckily, their name was also Steppel.

„Union" = und „Compromiss"=Nähzutaten sind praktisch und billig!

---

18. Passover
19. Visa

Gütermann & Co., Nähseiden-Fabriken, Gutach-Breisgau

They are good people, and through them we got the protection that others could not as easily achieve.[20]

But, the best of all is, that today, on my second day here, I already have a job. Yes, I actually have two offers.

I have packed the suitcase, and tomorrow I will move. How happy I am, that I will again have my own room and won't have to spend as much time looking for my belongings.

In our housing here, there is, at this time, a terrible disorder. Since we intend to move, nothing is being cleaned up. I was diligent in looking for a dwelling so that is how I found the job so quickly. We saw a sign "Room for Rent" in the Miliz Street.

Mr. Weimann is living there and my father introduced me to him. He asked us right there (in the street) if I would like to move into the house. He returned with us to our home, and his wife was satisfied. Tomorrow

---

20. Martin Gilbert, <u>The Macmillan Atlas of the Holocaust</u>, N.Y., 1982. "The local Belgium population was active in helping Jews, of whom 25,000 were hidden in private homes ... of the 25,630 Jews who were deported, only 1,244 survived." The destination of those deported, kept secret by the Nazis, was Auschwitz.

„Union" = und „Compromiss" =Nähzutaten sind praktisch und billig !

I will move in.

I thought it would be wonderful when moving in. After four weeks I moved out, disappointed.

One day later I accepted a job at a Flemish tailoress. The three weeks that I stayed with her were the most horrible in Antwerp. Whenever she was not insulting others, she scolded me, or vice versa. Then the vacations started in Antwerp.

The businesses were closed and I was free. I don't believe that anyone else has been able to work for her for this length of time, but I.

During the vacation I knitted for a store, and also made children's and baby clothing (privately) in order to earn some extra money.

Fourteen days later I finally got a job in Belgium where I stayed until the outbreak of the war (September, 1939). This was as a mother's helper. Despite my own troubles, the lady of the house was a very good soul, and I loved the children very much. They did everything to please me. This became apparent when I met with an accident while swimming. For four weeks I lay in bed, and all the food had to be brought to me.

The children did all they could do for me. Thus, all this time of waiting passed and the pain subsided.

Twice while I was there we traveled to Coxyde, near the sea, where the woman of the house had an apartment. A rumor was circulating that led us to believe that we might have to flee. Quite too soon, and much like a surprise,[21] this presentment was to be real.

1940, date unmarked

During the night from the 9th to the 10th of May, Germany, "The Dragon" suddenly invaded: Belgium, Holland, and Luxembourg! Now we must escape! Again!

On the same day (Friday) we saw thousands of Jewish refugees fleeing Antwerp. We decided to flee the following Wednesday. By then[22] most had already left the city, (since people saw that it was useless to resist the German advance). We realized that if we waited any later there would not be a possibility to escape. The Belgium soldiers do not even put up a fight against the

„Union" = und „Compromiss"=Nähzutaten sind praktisch und billig!

---

21. Without warning.
22. Friday

Germans. So, on Tuesday, we waited at the station for a train to take us out of here. When a train finally did arrive it was unbearably overcrowded with people, so we did not board.

We did not flee from Germany to live with Hitler in a foreign country.

Luckily, we got a camionette,[23] which took 30 people and us on our flight [24] away from these invaders.

I have not enough ink nor paper to describe all the details of it. Besides, I do not remember it that clearly any more.[25] Yet I know that it will not leave quickly from my memory.

---

23. This usually refers to a small bus.
24. Escape
25. As in earlier entries in her diary, Leah's "poor memory" could be a defense mechanism to safeguard her from the terrible memories and experiences.

„Union" = und „Compromiss" =Nähzutaten sind praktisch und billig!

Gütermann & Co., Nähseiden=Fabriken, Gutach~Breisgau

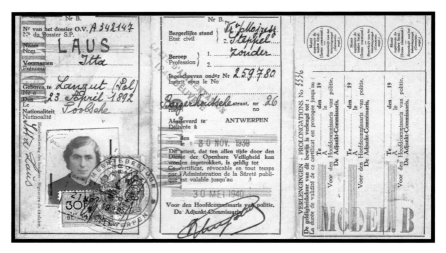

This is a tri-fold identification card carried by Itta after she and
Moses arrived in Antwerp. Leah talks about
presenting themselves to the police for purposes of
registering. This process was one of the first that
segregated Jews from the rest of the population.

„Union" = und „Compromiss" =Nähzutaten sind praktisch und billig !

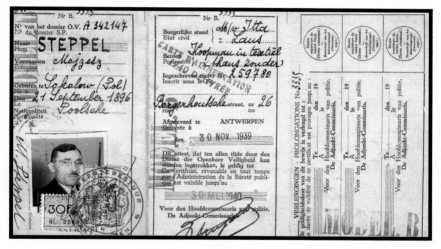

Tri-fold identification card carried by Moses after he
and Itta arrived in Antwerp.

„Union" = und „Compromiss" = Nähzutaten sind praktisch und billig!

September 1, 1940
Curia, Portugal

I will describe the trip to Curia in another entry. Today I will write something else. Something that should make every girl proud. It is a marriage proposal.

The first time (such) a proposal was made to me in Bordeaux. After a long journey[26] we arrived in Bordeaux, completely broken and dead tired. We did not know where to go. We were desperate. The men were allowed to stay overnight in the synagogue. The place was everything else but hygienic and clean. For the women staying there was completely impossible.

In the evening many members came to the synagogue. One of them invited me to sleep at her house until we could find lodging. It was her son (who liked me). He was very attentive towards me from the first moment he saw me. He was 20 years old and did everything for me.

„Union" = und „Compromiss" =Nähzutaten sind praktisch und billig!

---

26. The journey she just mentioned was from Antwerp to Bordeau. It is easy to become confused because Leah's entries bounce back and forth as she recalls experiences. Her list of places they stayed at helps sort out the time frames.

Gütermann & Co., Nähseiden=Fabriken, Gutach~Breisgau

I had only to point out what I wanted. He said he would even "fall out" with his family for me. Since I had nothing else to do, we met every day. He was, indeed, a very fine young man, and I understood him very well. Because of this he took our relationship seriously. He gave me a present, a lovely handkerchief, but this does not bring me any luck.

„Union" = und „Compromiss" =Nähzutaten sind praktisch und billig!

The Germans advance closer and closer. On one particular day we experienced two bombardments. The day before we had gotten the visas for Portugal and we were so exhausted. The deciding factor to leave came when my brother, whom we had not heard from in four weeks, (since his conscription into the French army), arrived home quite suddenly. I think of the handkerchief. The luggage was packed. Again, we had to start on our way, with the help of G-d.[27]

Step by step we made our way. Mostly, we traveled by foot. Occasionally, a vehicle would stop and take us for a short distance.

---

27. The following pages help unravel the confusion and complexities of the Steppel journey. Gratefully, Mother was meticulous in listing the cities, towns, and villages. On the other hand, the order in which she recalls and writes entries in her diary are not necessarily in orderly sequence. The countries that the Steppels journeyed through were in this order: Germany, The Netherlands (Holland), Belgium, France, Spain, and finally Portugal. Incredibly, they traversed the entire length of France! This is an incredible feat considering the great danger and distances At some points they were able to pass back and forth over borders because of their close proximity to the adjoining countries.

„Union" = und „Compromiss" =Nähzutaten sind praktisch und billig !

Step by step we made our way. Mostly, we traveled by foot. Occassionally, a vehicle would stop and take us for a short distance."

1. Düsseldorf
2a Heerlen
2b Aachen
3 Antwerp
4 The Hague
5 Pas de Calais
6 Abbeville
7 Paris
8 Bordeaux
9 Hendaye
10 Salamanca
11 Porto
12 Lisbon

The Steppels fled from Antwerp, Belgium to Lapan, Meenen, passing through Pas de Calais, which is located in the northernmost corner of France, near the Straits of Dover. Hendaye is located in the most southwest corner of France on the border near Spain. Troeport, Aubervilliers (she wrote 'Abbeville') are located near Paris, France.

Note: This map was conceived in 1996 with a WWII map and Leah's list on the following page (no Google, no computer).

ב"ה

Leah kept a detailed list of countries, cities and towns where she and her family stayed.

Key:
Tg. = day
Voch = week
Nacht = night (i.e., overnight stay)
Mon. = month

September, 1940

I arrived at Hendaye (in the Pyrennees region of France) dead tired. There I settled the remaining formalities, and we readied ourselves to cross the border. After a long wait at the French/Spanish border we came to Irun. Immediately upon entering this border town we saw what terrible results Spain had suffered from its long civil war. Most of the city was in ruins! Later, when we traveled in a slow train through Spain we saw what kind of poverty and destruction had befallen the country. This once beautiful, flourishing, and rich land was in shambles.

War destroys everything.
Why don't foolish people understand
that one can only lose; no one wins by
war.

In Salamanca, the last (Spanish) town before Portugal, we had to stay overnight. It was too late to continue and there were no trains leaving. Since we had slept at the train station at Irun, and I had not slept the two nights at Bayonne, I went to find lodging so we could all try to rest. People had recommended a place, saying it was inexpensive. We were all famished, and were excited to have found lodging,

Unfortunately, the food was inedible. We got stomach aches from the little bit we did eat. I must say, though, that we did have a restful night's sleep. Yet, we would not have relaxed so easily had we known beforehand the amount of the bill. It was six times the amount we had arranged (the night before). We returned to them that which they gave to us. We gave them one dollar and told them it had the value of sixty francs. They understood this to be the equivalent of ten pesetos, and were satisfied with it. So were we!

We came to Vilar Formoso at the Portuguese border. While in Spain, everything was tattered, dirty, and cold this time of year. At this border town it was different: warm, light, and clean. It gave the impression of a well organized country. We also had to remain here a day and a night. In the evening we saw a sight strange to us: men, women, and children gathering at a well in the middle of town. They were washing (themselves), shaving, cleaning their teeth, and combing their hair.

The next day each of us was called (by name) into the office and directed to go to a certain village or town. *This is how we come to be in Curia. Now we traversed Portugal. What a difference to Spain! Previously, we had not seen any planted fields. Here we passed flourishing gardens, clean villages, and rich fields. The village of Pampilhosa was the central railroad point and we had to change trains. Once again we need lodging. After the sleepless night in Vilar Formoso we yearned for a bed.*

Since we had had such bad experiences in Spain, I did not want to leave the area of the train station. I walked towards a building near the station. It was the house of the station chief. We were kindly received and actually entertained. Henni and I were permitted to stay there overnight. We felt that this was a display of the character and friendliness of the Portuguese. Soon afterward, they invited me to stay with them for the day, which I accepted a few days hence.

The son of the house fell at once in love with me after I spent two days with his sister. Later, he often came to Curia. He was a very fine young man and his sister is lovely. Conversation with him was difficult since he could not speak any French; soon he "fell on my nerves." Nevertheless, his family did a lot of good things for us.

„Union" = und „Compromiss" =Nähzutaten sind praktisch und billig !

163

Let me tell you about Curia. It is a very pretty little village. It has a beautiful park with exquisite palm trees,[28] several large hotels, and a number of smaller boarding houses. Many Portuguese people come here for their vacation. There is also a casino. Next to the largest hotel there is a swimming bath which is really very nice. This is where you can find me nearly every day. In general, it is not bad here in Curia.

Leah among the palm trees in Curia.

---

28. From the description of Curia, the photograph above was probably taken in front of one of the beautiful palm trees she mentions in this entry.

But, after two months here I am becoming bored. Such a little hamlet is too much for me. It is a daily repetition.

Goethe[29] wrote:
Everything can be endured well,
Except for too many days of happiness. [30]

---

29. The great 19th century German poet. Until Hitler invaded and her life was turned upside down, Mother's aspirations were to go to medical school. Although those dreams were dashed away, she continued to be a prolific reader, and self-taught in many areas.

30. Paraphrased from the German.

Henni Steppel

September 2, 1940

Now we were in Curia. We rented a room and are still here today. I did not have to do too much, so in the beginning I went into the town with my brother. Later, we found another amusement, the swimming bath (pool). The manager seemed to like me. He is a slim, handsome man. I was interested for a while, but when I danced with someone else at the casino he became angry. I soon thereafter ended my relation with him.

September 24, 1940

After this I met a man from Lisbon. At first he said he was a Jew, but later I found out that he descended from a Jewish family. I conversed with him, once I even danced with him. This, of course, made the manager angry again. I did not mind, since I wanted "to end" with him once and for all. This fellow from Lisbon was quite a famous tennis player who came to Curia to participate in a tennis master(y). I cannot believe that a person can fall in such great love as he fell in love with me. One evening I was invited to a dinner in the hotel. After the second glass of wine he said, "I'll take my life unless you marry me." I became very disturbed after this remark and he apologized. He admitted that he did not really know what he had said. Today, I am still corresponding with him. He tried diligently to get us permission to move to Lisbon. But this is a very difficult task and he could not carry it through.

In the meantime, I became acquainted with a group of people, among them two advocates[31] who are now working on my behalf. Let us see what they will achieve. One evening we all enjoyed a bottle of

---

31. Attorneys

„Union" = und „Compromiss" =Nähzutaten sind praktisch und billig!

champagne, and one of them, who was writing books for the theater, said, "Let us arrange a revue of (our) youth." First, it was regarding our own lives, then it evolved into a great mystery revue. Today there is going to be an encore performance, because it was very successful. The author came from Lisbon especially for the performance. For my sake, he made the second showing with personal warmth. I know he took this opportunity to come to see me in Curia.

October, 1940
Curia

Oh, how cold it has become and so sadly desolate and empty. Just now I remember the old children's song that tells of the departure of the summer. But, it is not perchance. It is really desolate and empty. The leaves have fallen off the trees, one after another. Soon they will stand bare. And just like the leaves, one friend after another went back. Now it is completely different. I remember when it [32] was celebrated with song and dances: but now the cities are swept clean, with great noise, with motorcades.

At that time, the great author and director of music, Manuel, was picked up at the train station in order to play the review, "Mysteria." It was previously directed by him with great success. This second performance was much more brilliant and even more successful. I believe that because of me he suggested to repeat the review. [33]

---

32. A transition time like our Labor Day.
33. I believe this is further reference/background to the aforementioned.

169

He spent one hour with me to talk seriously. He asked me about religion and I told him about my religion. He also told me about his. He said that if a poor person (or someone in need of help) knocks at his office, then he does not ask if he needs money. He gives to the poor people, and he does not let his right hand slow down.[34] He never told this to anybody and he wanted to show me that our religions aren't so different as they appear; that he himself was a good person. He showed great interest in me and therefore he listened to everything I said (whatever he could extract from me). He said that everything is being revenged on earth.

---

34. Sounds like Leah was a bit too naive to smooth-talking techniques.

„Union" = und „Compromiss" =Nähzutaten sind praktisch und billig!

When the tennis player was here and they saw me often together with him, they started to talk about me.[35] People talk in great detail because they knew me.

If someone is bad himself, he also thinks badly of other people.[36]

I did not consider that I was in Portugal. I see that the goose is of a supernatural kind of sensual temperament. I have never done anything improper or undignified. When I later went to Lisbon, Curia was a done deal for me. The real reason to go to Lisbon is that I wanted to achieve something for my parents at the foreign consulate. I could not go very far with this and only an application was completed. Our whole family was trying to move there.

Three weeks later, this application was denied.

---

35. Leah found herself the focus of gossip. The following sections are steeped in innuendo and somewhat difficult to follow. She never quite spells out the situations entirely. The gist and her philosophical outlook are enlightening.

36. One of my mother's favorite axioms: Don't speak unfavorably about another's bad habits because it's probably one of your own.

„Union" = und „Compromiss"=Nähzutaten sind praktisch und billig!

Since I was there (for once), I was amusing myself: I visited an exhibition, toured Lisbon, and went swimming in the ocean. All of this was in public. I do not think evil, nor did I do anything that is not proper. People have nothing to do, so they talk!

They do not know that evil and untruth can kill a person.[37]

I came the next day to the Palace Hotel to talk to Manuel. He had told me he would do everything to help us go to Lisbon (when he was here the first time), and I had to tell him that our request was denied.

The day of my leave-taking Manuel disappeared and I remained in the company of his friends. He had asked about my plans. I told him we were still waiting to go to Lisbon, He told me that our name was already known by the police.

He knew the Director of the jail and he would speak in our behalf. On September 23rd he promised to write to tell us of any results; to this day I have not heard from him,

---

37. Throughout my childhood years I can honestly say I never heard my mother gossip.

I thought (until now) that these people were good friends,

I now know I can only rely on myself and G-d.

From bad experiences you become wise. I'm waiting daily for mail. Even the tennis player does not write. Time will show if I'm pessimistic or realistic. The time of the year does lend itself to hope. It is cold. It is rainy. There is no company in the village. If I think about it (that it's possible to remain here all winter long), I could despair.

Would could I do? I could either embroider all day long, I could write, I could talk to the farmers, or go to the post office. Also, with the commissioner, I can not talk too much, as he has become too personal towards me. And the war continues. There is no end to the suffering of mankind. Who knows what is written in the Book of Fate for me? I thought about this when we were still happy, after much sufferings in Belgium, and we said good-bye there. Then in the middle of May we came to France, to the border there. We did not find any vehicle to continue our travels. We went by foot and only had a wagon with a dog (in front). A man was happily walking along showing us the way to the border of France.

On the way, my brother had the idea to cross over the train tracks for an auto stop, but I did not think that this was a wise idea. One could see vehicles criss-crossed along the tracks and I was against this entirely. We asked instructions of the chaplain in the village of Aachen.[38]

He said he was going that way and we could accompany him.[39] So we went along with him and we decided to meet again at the railway station. We arrived at that place and I became too anxious, so I went back a little bit to wait on the highway.

I sat down alongside, on the grass, and I happily ate orange pieces, one after another.

Suddenly, a fear gripped me. I jumped up and asked the first bicyclist I saw if he had seen a wagon coming from Meenen and I described my parents to him. He had not seen anything of that sort and I was nearly in despair.

---

38. A border village that is in the approximate triangular meeting point of the borders of Belgium, Holland, and Germany, but also close to France.

39. Apparently at this point Leah went in a different direction than her parents or on ahead.

„Union" = und „Compromiss" =Nähzutaten sind praktisch und billig!

When I learned that there is a different highway from which they could have turned, I quickly went back to the train station and there, from far away, I saw that my brother and father were walking but accompanied by policemen with drawn revolvers! No one can imagine my thoughts at that time.

I did not make myself seen, but went around the station to gather information. I was able to learn that when my parents arrived at the train station they were unable to find me. Thereupon, my father and brother, anxious with fright and despair, ventured into the village itself to look for me.

They could not, I might add, speak any French. They were also rather conspicuous. So they were stopped by German paratroopers.

I was able to talk our way out of this potential disaster. [40]

Luckily for us there were English military in this village. I told them of my suffering and they promised to help. After a short wait a truck came and they didn't ask many questions of us. They loaded our baggage onto the truck.

---

40. One can only surmise, that with blond hair and blue eyes, Leah was able to present herself as Aryan and concoct "stories."

„Union" = und „ Compromiss" =Nähzutaten sind praktisch und billig !

Now our travels went a little quicker. Two kilometers from the border the driver said that he would have to cross by himself. The bags were unloaded and we were left there.

We, however, were not disheartened. We placed our faith in our lucky star, which had helped us until then. There was a long line of other trucks and vehicles.

I went one by one asking if anyone had a place for us. This did not happen, though. I found a vehicle with young people who were willing to take our baggage. Thus, we went over the border to France by foot. We continued to Neux Chapel and then on to Locon.[41]

We were kept safe and housed in farmhouses. The people were friendly and very compassionate towards us. Now it was impossible to continue from Locon. The Germans came, always advancing more and more, and waiting in this village was simply too much for us. My brother and I, we made a plan. We traveled five kilometers into the next village by bicycle to try and gain some news.

---

41. See Page 160 for the list of the towns, villages and cities Leah fled to and through.

„Union" = und „Compromiss" =Nähzutaten sind praktisch und billig !

We made a contact, we learned that there would be a train leaving from there. I found and spoke to a Jewish family and they suggested that we go to Paris. They so generously also gave me one hundred francs.

It is so difficult to obtain a vehicle. Other than military transport, there is no means of transportation. But, on the next day, gratefully, we did make a connection to use a military transport.

October 10, 1940

In the morning it seemed to me that it would be a very dark, rainy, November-like day, as I was accustomed to from Belgium. My heart was also dark. Now, about an hour later, the sun appeared, quite unexpectedly. So I thought that there will soon come a time when the sun will shine for me. It is good to hope. I hope that this truly dark section of my life will pass and the leaf will turn and show its lighter side. Even so, we should never be thankless.

How was it at that time that we pushed like animals in a cattle car, and traveled to an uncertain future? We were open and vulnerable to the bombs of our enemies. There were constant alerts. The trains would stop and the announcement "Everyone get off!" We would then have to find and take another train. We never knew where the next train would bring us.

Once, when we were near Abbeville we just narrowly escaped the danger of death. By a great miracle, like a wonder, we found a place to stay (hide) in a wagon. The next day I came upon an awful bombardment. In the terrible, frenzied situation, many people lost their lives and others their belongings.

178

Gütermann & Co., Nähseiden-Fabriken, Gutach-Breisgau

And thus, we traveled from one place to the next, never knowing where (we) would be next. So it went until we reached Paris. We remained three days in Paris because we were so tired and assumed we would likely remain there.

But, a call came out: All refugees must leave the city! We didn't hesitate at all. We quickly decided to make our way to Bordeaux.[42]

Unfortunately, I led the family into the military barracks, from where I believed we would be evacuated. There my brother, Paul, was immediately arrested to do work and be educated for the military. So, we stayed in Bordeaux longer than anticipated: about four weeks. I already mentioned what happened to us then.

Now, we are here in Curia, and we are here for three months already and we had not had intentions of staying here for even 30 days.

---

42. Approximately 500 miles southeast of Paris, along the French seacoast, and about 125 miles from the Spanish border.

„Union" = und „Compromiss" = Nähzutaten sind praktisch und billig !

October 14,1940
Curia

I do not understand the mentality of the Portuguese people. Yesterday, because of a little "nothing" there was a brawl between them. Perhaps, they drink too much wine. Only wine and women can affect the minds of these Portuguese men and arise them from their drowsiness. If you ask something of them, they respond, "Never." They do not do anything immediately, unless you push them. It's very hard to stir them from their lethargy.

Also, I believe, that they have not forgotten me in Lisbon. But, do they write? Nada – Never.

The Portuguese are not bad. To the contrary. One just cannot be hasty with them. One must talk to them and stay close to them.[43]

---

43. She always said: "You can get more with honey, than with vinegar." It appears she learned her "lessons" early in life and their impressions were lasting ones.

December 8, 1940
Porto, Portugal

Again, another part of my life is closed: Curia. It was actually very pleasant. I learned about people; yet I move on.

Here in Porto, there is nothing of importance and I have learned more about disappointments. I imagined that those whom I considered my friends would do more. Some have done a little bit. Sometimes I even went to the movies. I was picked up by a good friend from Curia; the family have done many friendly gestures for me. Here I have no one because people live very far apart.

Now, I hope that my life will take a different route here. I have in my sights the idea of getting a few students whom I will teach English and German.[44]

Firstly, this will help earn a little money. Secondly, it gives content to my days here. Next week I will learn more about the prospects.

Today is my 20th birthday – "a beautiful age" someone told me yesterday (whom I told about it). Looking

---

44. By this time Leah's repertoire of languages also included French, Polish, Hebrew (to read), and Yiddish.

„Union" = und „Compromiss" =Nähzutaten sind praktisch und billig!

back over the past year I have to remark that I never had such a colorful and changing year! How many disappointments, how many destroyed hopes! But, if I take the accounting, everything is bad. Who knows where we will be next year on my birthday. Maybe under better conditions. That is my birthday wish!

These are my thoughts on my birthday:

Other people are happy on their birthday getting presents and celebrating the day in the circle of their friends and acquaintances. They do not reflect for a moment on what has happened before or what will occur in the future.

January 12, 1941

A new year has begun and I hope it will bring more happiness and joy than the past one. It is already one month since I last wrote in my diary.

I spend time thinking about the contents of my days. I am now a real lady professor. I have students in English, German and French. To think that just one short year ago I spoke not one word of French. In any case, I teach French to children. The German and English students are men. So far, it goes quite well.

I have a story to recount about this class because it makes me secure and proud of myself. It is well known that the Portuguese love foreigners. The only negative is that I usually have to wait for them. One day, while waiting, I showed the stenographer some of my pictures. At that time a male student came in, and took and kept two of the pictures. I only realized it the following day. I wrote a note asking for the return of my photos. When he returned to class, he denied it, stubbornly. I was quite mad, yet I did have trouble containing my laughter during the hour.

At the end of class, I took a different tact, and said in quite a changed tone, " Please, give me back my photos and I will give you the best one and everything will be as it was before. "

Of course, previously he had sworn he had anything of mine. Now, he reached for his satchel.

"Now, I am really a liar," he said, as he returned the photos to me.

I had compassion for him, his tone was so sad.

"I have already forgotten the whole thing," I said, as I handed him the best of the lot.

January 19, 1941

At this time of great excitement and nervousness I am quickly reaching for my pen to write down a few trains of thought. The general theme of conversation today is about "The American Consulate" and the Consul himself. The moment has come when everybody tries his luck with the Consul, and whomsoever is lucky will go home with the visa in his pocket.

Recently, I am spending much time amongst us Jews. Formerly I thought we Jews are a small, wretched people, and there was reason to hate us. Today, I must change my mind: we are a good-hearted group. We rightfully call ourselves "the chosen people." What I now see is willingness to sacrifice and help each other unselfishly. This I say, cannot be found anywhere else. Perhaps in future days one [45] might write about it, and you will read about this yourselves.

---

45. In fact, many years later, Eli Wesel and other writers did pay homage to the tenacity and dignity of the courageous "chosen people."

Gütermann & Co., Nähseiden=Fabriken, Gutach~Breisgau

Everyone tries to help the other and advise him what to do. Now everyone can obtain an American visa. But you need money, you need so much money which one person alone cannot procure. But altogether they put all the money together and every day another person can go with enough money to the consulate. We exchange our experiences. Those who were strangers to each other just the day before, today they trust each other. They talk about their sorrows and troubles. People who were never connected are now trusting each other with their money. Now, even humor gets through.

"The Consul was whistling today during the negotiations," one remarked. "Oh, when he whistles, everything is in order."

Another says, "How rich everybody suddenly is, they only talk thousands of dollars." We get among the diplomats and our conversation relates to the Consul. The proof: Consul, evidence, dollars, = visa. Further jokes are: "How can I sleep when someone else has my money?"

January 28, 1941

Since I wrote the previous entry, I must state that I regret having done it. Our supposedly best friends put stones in our path, and they held back those who were inclined to help us. To be true, they had difficulties themselves. They did not succeed in their plan therefore they don't want us to try the same. G-d helped us, as He always helps the downtrodden, and finally we found a few who were willing to assist us. Tomorrow, with G-d's help, we will venture and take the big step to acquire a visa. We hope to show those who have begrudged us that in spite of them, we succeed.

Last night I dreamed. This dream is especially important to me because since my childhood, I have never dreamed such a lively and clear dream. It remained distinct in my memory.

I dreamed that I went with a girl comrade (who happened to be disliked by others), and whom I myself did not like. I clearly recalled her name and appearance. We passed a sandy and grown-over spot, and I knew that something had been hidden there. She tried to dissuade me from staying there, however, I succeeded

„Union" = und „Compromiss" =Nähzutaten sind praktisch und billig!

in digging at this spot. I found a gold ring[46] with a lilac colored stone in its center and surrounded with points of gold.

Additionally, I also found a wristwatch but it did not work because the sand had gotten into it. The watch had a golden band and a very small dial plate. A little square was showing on which I could read the time. Of course, the envious girl immediately recognized the value of the ring.

I put the ring on my finger. However, she wanted me to give it to her, but I merely laughed. She only learned about the watch when I gave it to a watchmaker. He asked me if he should fix it. I answered in the affirmative. She interrupted me and said, "No don't fix it, it will be too expensive."

When asking her what she had to do with this matter, she replied, "The watch belongs to me since you have the ring for yourself." The watchmaker scolded her thoroughly, whereupon she disappeared.

---

46. Leah drew a picture of a small ring in this entry. Years later, of course, Mother made her livelihood as a jewelry designer and manufacturer. She was a specialist in cut stones, pearls, gold, and diamonds and often drew her ideas in a little book.

Gütermann & Co., Nähseiden=Fabriken, Gutach~Breisgau

February 5, 1941

So, as my father would say, we risked it. We had gone to the American Consul. All our anxieties were relieved. We were well received and no tricky questions were asked of us. I assume that we made a good impression. Unfortunately, we only presented with a small sum of money. We were asked to return in fourteen days; eight have already gone by. Once again we pray for good luck that we will be received well and be successful. That is the American business.[47]

Regarding my lessons, which had been going steadily upwards, now it rapidly declines. One cannot count on the Portuguese. In the beginning they were all enthusiastic; the one who was the most ardent gave it up. Surely, the others will follow.

Na, we hope to leave soon anyway, and I won't regret anything here. Meanwhile, I hope to shop cheaply. If possible, directly from the manufacturer. I have already ordered a blouse. I found a pair of shoes,

---

47. This is so much the "flavor" of Mother's style that I hesitate to change it. She was obviously writing in brevity to get on to the next paragraph and discuss her bargains.

„Union" = und „Compromiss" =Nähzutaten sind praktisch und billig !

Gütermann & Co., Nähseiden=Fabriken, Gutach~Breisgau

which I bought "direct" and they were quite cheap and a great value. I never thought I'd find a pair of shoes to fit. This shopping spree I like.[48]

It does not pay to be too sensitive. The Portuguese don't deserve it.

---

48. Some things are universal! It was refreshing to read about some lighthearted subject matter like shopping.

2018 Note: I inherited Leah's shoe shopping gene!

„Union"= und „Compromiss"=Nähzutaten sind praktisch und billig!

February 19, 1941
Portugal

Yesterday we were at the American Consulate to try our luck. I believe that our fortune does not lie in America, since it is impossible for us to get there. The Consul denied our visa application. I asked the Secretary to get permission from the Consul to let me speak to him personally. This was also denied. Thereupon, I spoke to the vice-consul, since I was used at the consulate as an interpreter. He did, in fact, talk to the Consul himself about our case. This turned out to be of no use either. Now, we must obtain a new affidavit, or America is OVER .

From the beginning I thought we would be unsuccessful. Whenever I pictured everything nice and fine, and felt matters would go well, things went wrong. I always had to catch myself dreaming, and then I know it is over. I am always mad at myself, but I can't help it.

By the way, I observed that the American Consulate does stare at me when I am there, and does enjoy talking to me. I believe he certainly would help if he could.

But, he is merely the mouthpiece for the Consul himself. He must pass on the word from above, and it is usually bad news. The good news the Consul will tell them himself.

Last week there was a violent storm in Portugal. It was such a severe storm the likes of which had not been experienced here in fifty years. Hundreds died; many were injured. Many millions in property were destroyed or damaged. The next day we could see the storm's devastation and destruction. The streets were full of bricks and broken glass. The strongest trees were cracked like matches. It was a wild sight!

If a storm can do so much destruction, how much more desolation will be caused by the war which increases daily and continues endlessly.

March 9, 1941

Since my last entries (in this diary) some time has passed. Many things have occurred in the meantime. Most important, I can report that finally, finally, we received approval for the affidavit. It came with much trouble and took much time, I could hardly believe it myself. It was like a miracle to me.

The way it happened was different than usual. We were there (at the Consulate) the last time our matter had been denied. We did not have enough money. So we had to get money. But that was easy in those days. You walk into a jeweler's store and obtain a certificate that jewelry in the value of so and so much was sold to that customer. With some luck we succeeded to get such a sales ticket. We also received a written estimate of the value of the[49] *diamonds. Then we went to work! It meant to procure money. You have to show the money to the Consul.*

We could not obtain the money from our good friends. I did not want to wait several weeks again as the time before. I had the courage to approach a man not well known to us. He was, of course, very angry, how I could ask him. But I got it! [50]

For two days I visited all our acquaintances, I didn't even have time to eat. On Tuesday, February 29th, there was a carnival. On that day we went to the Consul and he took away our papers and we were informed that we would be getting the decision in writing. Our disappointment was great.

We had had so much trouble to obtain the money, and now no success. We had to accept this answer and wait.

---

49. The word "the" is reference to diamonds that they left Germany with and held onto for just such an opportunity.

50. How enlightening if Leah had spelled out how she convinced this man.

Two days later, on Thursday, we heard from a person who had been at the Consul that he saw, at the office of the vice-consul stamped papers with the name "Steppel." He said it might not be ours, probably someone else's. Our case seemed to him in "bad light."

This news made me go up to the Consul myself. The secretary received me with the words,

"I have some good news for you. I spoke immediately to the Vice-Consul and I received a note for the doctor."[51] I was greatly surprised, nobody could believe it. The news spread like wildfire. Our friends were happy with us, and those envious of us felt angry. We, however, thanked G-d for His wonderful help.

---

51. Unfortunately, the reference to the "doctor" can only be surmised to be the O.K. for an examination before visa final approval.

Gütermann & Co., Nähseiden=Fabriken, Gutach~Breisgau

Tuesday
March 11, 1941
With G-d's Help

We received the Visa! Now, that part is settled. This does not mean that we are in America yet. The next remaining obstacle is to look for a ship. I went to all the ship companies; only one held out a possible prospect. There is no certainty in this matter; even they do not know which ships will sail. Thus, we have to continue trusting in G-d. He always led us miraculously. We have confidence in Him. He will continue to lead us.

„Union" = und „Compromiss"=Nähzutaten sind praktisch und billig!

Gütermann & Co., Nähseiden=Fabriken, Gutach~Breisgau

April 4, 1941

I am just reading the last verses about trust in our G-d.[52] I feel that I was doing right to depend upon our Father (in Heaven) and I promise to do this all through my life. Only He will help us.

I am sitting here on a train to Lisbon. My parents will follow within a week. Then, G-d willing, we will travel to America on the ship "Nyassa."[53] I do have, unfortunately, an obstacle to report: so far we only have three ship tickets. I hope to get the two missing ones in Lisbon. I am not worrying too much about it. It will probably be very difficult; but I am sure to succeed.

---

52. Leah does not mention which verses she is reading. I will venture a conjecture at two possibilities: T'hillim (Psalms) or Pirkei Avot (Wisdom of the Fathers). The latter contains classic thoughts on moral philosophy and righteous conduct. The former, the more familiar Psalms, was a comfort to Mother all through her life. Both are small, powerful volumes that are concealable and transportable.

53. Or Nysissa; at this printing the exact name and information about this has not been researched. Mother often referred to the ship that brought her to the United States as a "banana boat."
2018 Note: Nyassa

„Union" = und „Compromiss" =Nähzutaten sind praktisch und billig!

197

This is the second time that I travel to Lisbon. The first time we went to the Hizem (Jewish Aid Society) in Lisbon to get money for the tickets. At the Hizem, we had some difficult experiences. The first time we were received poorly. We were in despair, walking around like a "chicken without its head." One gentleman who saw us in such a condition, approached us and advised us to go into another building of the Hizem.

Should we encounter difficulties there, he told us to turn to a couple he knew well. We should introduce ourselves by giving them "regards from Dr. Redlich."

We went to this couple and found the woman especially charming. She tried very hard to bring us in contact with persons with authority. The gentleman spoke softly to us, with kind words of encouragement. This has given us a lilitle more hope.

I stayed at the Frankfort Hotel with my girlfriend with whom I had also stayed at The Palace Hotel in Curia. We slept there and ate dinner together.

A certain man from the Hizem used to come by the hotel frequently to visit a sick friend. Mrs. Almeida[54]

---

54. The charming lady she just wrote about?

introduced me to him and I spent time explaining our situation. He promised to do his utmost in our matter. I can only surmise the above, because two days later the money was in Porto! We were now able to pay for the three ship tickets. I hope matters about the missing two tickets will also work out. This is presently my greatest worry. As always, I believe, G-d will not abandon us, as He has never abandoned us before.

I hope to continue my next notes aboard the ship, since I will presumably have little time in Lisbon.

I have forgotten to mention one occurrence since it is very interesting and I do not want to miss telling about it. It happened on March 11th. We were at the American Consulate to pick up our visas.

The employee who was writing out our visas said, "I have to talk to you. It's urgent. However, we cannot talk here. We'll have to talk at your place."

He seemed to indicate that it was something very unpleasant and we were in a dangerous situation.[55]

At this turning point, I was no longer happy about the visas. I was thoroughly distracted by what we may be told by this employee. I could hardly contain myself.

When he finally did come, he explained how unsure our situation was at that time. Someone had gone to the American Consulate to betray us by saying we were unworthy.

Thank G-d, he met this fine young gentleman, who did not pass this rumor on to the Consul himself.

He told us that the consulate receives many anonymous letters of all sorts. But, the consul, who is an honest man, puts these aside. He knows that each case must be dealt with on its own merits.

---

55. Mother had often eluded to "helping" others and themselves with document preparation in order to hasten or gain freedom.

„Union" = und „Compromiss" =Nähzutaten sind praktisch und billig!

DAILY MIRROR SATURDAY APRIL 26

(Mirror)

Otylia Lea Steppel (left), 20, and sister, Henny, 15, refugees from Poland. They lived in French train for 10 weeks.

A newspaper clipping of Leah and her sister, Henni, in the *New York Daily Mirror*. The date that can be seen is April 26, year unknown, but it is quite certain that she was older than 20.* Even among the sea of refugees that flowed through Ellis Island, somehow my mother attracted attention from the media. The caption reads:

> "Otylia Lea Steppel (left), 20, and sister, Henni, 15,
> refugees from Poland. They lived
> in French train for 10 weeks."

* RB 2018 note: We are certain the year was 1941. We now know she ported in Brooklyn, N.Y.

Jan. 9.1947

I had an awful dream last night. It seemed as if everybody was picking on me and taken pot shots at me, but everybody. I was running on the street, and from all sides people were shooting at me, because I am a Jew, others, who I recognized as being Jewish themselves, shot at me because they wanted the pin I was wearing. girls and boys alike, finally I came to a place, I went inside, there were too girls, I said: Please don't do anything to me anymore, I can't take it anymore they said: no, we won't come inside. Inside was a big hall,

Above and following page: This "dream scene" entry is the only one written in English. Now married to Jacob, Lea Dykan was haunted by night terrors. It is interesting to note that she was also pregnant with her first child (and most probably did not know this yet.)
Line 14: too girls = two girls

Gütermann & Co., Nähseiden-Fabriken, Gutach-Breisgau

Tables said like for a wedding
or big party, a woman was
sitting on the side, I sort of felt
safe. I had to sound casual
not to show how frightend
and exhausted I was, so
I said: Oh, how nice.
But this was to much for
me. This sense of wellbeing
and "nice" was more than
I could stand, so I collapsed
were I was standing I cried
like my heart was breaking
I woke up than with tears
streaming down my face.

Warnung vor Nachahmungen! • Nur echt mit Firma Gütermann & Co.

Line I: Table said = set
Line 8 : to = too
Line 11 : could = could not

After rain
Comes sunshine.
After winter
Spring,
After sorrow
Joy.
Therefore, you
must never
be discouraged, but
must always hope for
Happiness.

Leah Steppel

This last entry, written in English, was found on a separate slip of paper, nestled in between the last pages of the second diary. It is a beautiful testimony of Leah's strong commitment to living life well and with optimism. The legacy she left for her children and grandchildren is for all people who cherish human dignity.

May 25, 1996
R.D.B.

204

Life
begins

in
America

Central Park, New York City, 1944

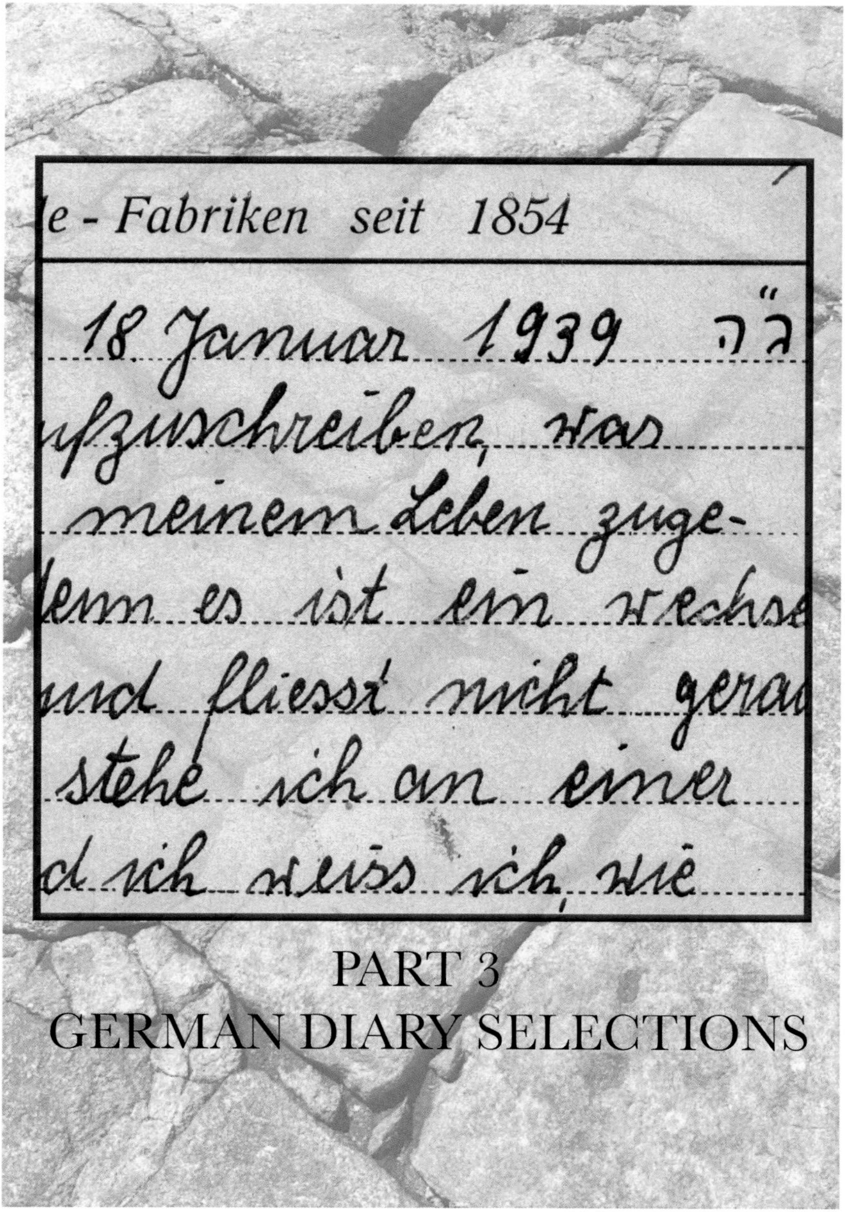

e - Fabriken   seit   1854

18 Januar 1939 ב"ה

fzuschreiben, was

meinem Leben zuge-

enn es ist ein wechse

und fliesst nicht gera

stehe ich an einer

d ich weiss ich, wie

PART 3
GERMAN DIARY SELECTIONS

Nähseide - Fabriken seit 1854

Heute, am 18 Januar 1939 ב"ה
beginne ich aufzuschreiben, was
sich alles in meinem Leben zuge-
tragen hat, denn es ist ein wechsel-
volles Leben und fliesst nicht gerade
dahin. Jetzt stehe ich an einer
Biegung, und ich weiss ich, wie
es dahinter aussieht.
Meine Jugend war ziemlich eintönig.
Mit 7 Jahren wanderten ich mit meinen
Eltern und Geschwister von Polen aus
und zogen nach Düsseldorf
Bis zum Jahre 1933 ging alles glatt
und eintönig. Meine Eltern arbeiteten
schwer und sauer für das tägliche
Brot. Da gefiel es G"tt uns Juden zu
strafen und sandte einen zweiten
Haman. Jetzt ging das Leben in
Angst und Sorge um die Zukunft
weiter. Man wusste nicht, was morgen

This page and following page: Leah's handwriting is ramrod straight
and controlled. She is confident in her writing and exhibits poise.

kommt und es bestand auch keine
Möglichkeit, fortzufahren.
Ich schrieb an unsere Verwandten
in Amerika, das war im April 1938.
Solange zögerten wir, denn wir hofften
immer, es wird besser werden.
Sie schickten uns eine bejahende
Antwort und versprachen, alles für
uns zu tun, was möglich ist.
Dann fing das grösste Unglück
an. Alle polnischen Juden mussten
Deutschland verlassen. Abends, punkt
12 Uhr im Oktober des Jahres 1938
klopfte es an unserer Tür (ich selbst
war z. Z. im Krankenhaus) die Polizei
stand draussen und begehrte Einlass.
Sie forderten meine Eltern auf,
alles, was wertvoll ist zusammen-
zupacken und mitzukommen. Sie
erklärten, meine Eltern würden

48

Amann's Nähseide in 1000 Farben

zuspielen. Wie kann man sich
nur so verlieben, wie er sich
in mich verliebt hat. Einmal
war ich in Luso; einer Meister-
schaft die er mitgemacht hat
beizuwohnen, des abends war
ich eingeladen bei dem Diner im
Hotel. Nach dem 2. Glas weissem
Wein wusste er nicht mehr
was er sagte: „Ich werde mir das
Leben nehmen, wenn Du mich
nicht heiratest." sagte er. Da ich
danach sehr böse wurde, ent-
schuldigte er sich oftmals und
gab zu, nicht zu wissen was er
sagte. Heute stehe ich noch
immer in Briefwechsel mit ihm.
Er hat viel versucht, uns eine
Erlaubnis zu verschaffen, nach
Lissabonne zu kommen. Doch

This page and following page: Leah's handwriting is "heavier," and perhaps rushed.

ist dies eine sehr schwierige
Angelegenheit und konnte er
es nicht durchsetzen.
Inzwischen bin ich hier im
Hotel mit einer Gesellschaft
bekanntgeworden und zwar
sind da auch 2 Advokaten
bei, die jetzt für mich arbei-
ten. sehen wir was sie tuen
können. Eines Tages saßen wir alle
sie bei einer Flasche Champagner
und so sagte der eine, der viele
Bücher für Theater auch schreibt Lassen
wir eine Revue der Jugend veranstal-
ten. Zuerst war es nur etwas für
uns. später ist es eine grosse "Revue
Misterie" geworden. Heute sind sie
niederholt da sie grossen Erfolg hatte.
Der Autor kam speziel aus Lisabon
ihr zuliebe machte er die Niederholung
Warum: die Liebe hat auch ihm ...

diese Gelegenheit nach Evoria zu kommen

zu müsse ... geschlagen -

211

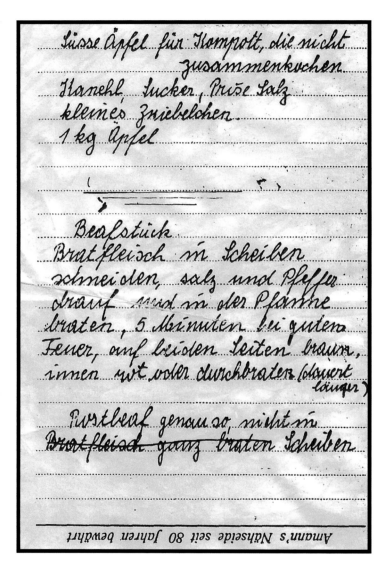

Süsse Äpfel für Kompott, die nicht
zusammenkochen.
Kanehl, Zucker, Prise Salz
kleines Zwiebelchen.
1 kg Äpfel

—————

Beafstück
Bratfleisch in Scheiben
schneiden, salz und Pfeffer
drauf und in der Pfanne
braten, 5 Minuten bei gutem
Feuer, auf beiden Seiten braun,
innen rot oder durchbraten (dauert
länger)

Rostbeaf genau so, nicht in
~~Bratfleisch ganz~~ braten Scheiben

Recipes from Leah's diary, on this page and the next page, are translated on page 214.

Möhren (Wurzeln)

1½ kg Möhren   (f. 5 Personen

etwas Fett

Prise Salz,

½ ons (50 gr) Zucker (ungefähr)

Wasser,

1½ - 2 Stunden kochen

Sauerkraut

1 kg Sauerkraut

Wasser,   1½ Stunden kochen

Fett, etwas mehr als bei Möhren,

dann Kartoffelbrei und durcheinanderstampfen

Pfeffer

Kochzeit 1½ - 2 Stunden

      Rote Kohl

½ Kopf rote Kohl

ung. 1 à 2 Äpfel

Fett

Pfeffer, Teelöfel Salz, Schüpe Zucker

wenn es fertig ist etwas Mehl, Kochzeit 2 Stunden

213

Recipes

(We can see from the following recipes that Leah is quite the novice when it comes to cooking. Translated from pages 212 and 213)

Susse Apfel (umlaut over a and u)
Sweet Apples for Compote
1 Kilo (about 2 pounds) apples that don't cook down (and get mushy)
Add sugar, pinch of salt, Canehl (a cinnamon from Ceylon), and 1 onion!

Beafstück
Beefsteak
Cut beef in slices, put on salt and pepper
fry in frying pan 5 minutes high/medium until both sides brown,
inside red or get it well done (takes longer)

Mohren (umlaut over the o)(carrots or root vegetables)
For 5 people
3 lbs. of carrots, small amount of fat, salt,
Add potato and mix well
1 ounce sugar
Cook 2 hours

Rote Kohl
Red Cabbage
1/2 head red cabbage
1-1 1/2 apples
Fat, pepper, salt, scoop of sugar
When done a little bit of flour
2 hours cooking time

214

schen Familie. Man riet mir
nur, nach Paris zu fahren.
Man gab mir auch 700 frank.
Nun hiess es ein Fahrzeug
bei bekommen, es waren nur
Militär-Fahrzeuge da, also fragte
ich einen Offizier und richtig
stand am anderen Tag ein
Militär-Wagen zu unserer
Verfügung.
10. Oktober 1940 :
Des Morgens schien es mir, als
würde es ein trüber regnerischer
November tag, so wie ich es von
Belgium gewohnt war, und trüb
war auch mein Herz, jetzt aber 1 Stunde
später ist der Sonnenschein durchge-
brochen, ganz unerwartet.
Vielleicht sind auch für mich bald :

On this and the following page we can see Leah's handwriting has a much less even tone. The date, 10. Oktober 1940, is in the middle of the page. Also noticeable are locations such as Paris, Belgium and Abbeville.

die Sonne scheinen. Es ist so gut zu hoffen, sicher wird auch dieser trübe Abschnitt vorüber- gehen, das Blatt wird sich wen- den und eine helle lichte Seite mit Freuden wird beginnen. Aber undankbar darf man seinem Schicksal nicht sein, wie ging es uns damals, als wir, wie das liebe Vieh zusam- mengepfercht in einem Bagag. waggon der ungewissen Zu- kunft entgegenfuhren, den Bomben der Feinde ausgesetzt, alle paar Minuten: "Alerte". Bei jeder Station, : "Alles aussteigen". Einen anderen Zug nehmen. Man wusste nicht, wo der andere Zug hinging. Zumal es war in Abbeville,

Am Dienstag den 11. März bekommen wir mit Gottes Hilfe das Visum. Dann ist diese Tappe erledigt doch damit sind wir noch nicht in Amerika. Jetzt hebt der trouble an mit einem Schiff. Ich war bei allen Schiffsgesellschaften und hat uns eine einzigste etwas in aussicht gestellt. Bisher ist es garnicht. Sie wissen es selbst noch nicht. Also muss man weiter auf Gottes Hilfe bauen, wie bisher, er hat uns immer wunderbar geführt. Wir vertrauen ihm! Er wird uns weiter führen.

6.4.1941. Ich lese gerade die letzten Aufzeichnungen vom

This and following page: 6.4.1941 (April 6, 1941) Leah appears rushed, harried, and perhaps writing while in a moving vehicle.

217

Gottvertrauen und sage
ich habe gut getan, auf
unseren Vater zu vertrau-
en und werde das mein Le-
ben lang tun. Er allein
hilft uns. Ich sitze hier
im Zug und fahre nach
Lissabon. Die Eltern werden
im Laufe der Woche nachkom-
men. Am 15. April fahren wir
dann mit Gottes Hilfe mit
dem Schiff "Kyoresa" nach
Amerika. Wir haben erst
3 Karten, doch hoffe ich die
anderen fehlenden 2 jetzt in
Lissabon zu erhalten. Ich
mache mir keine grosse
Illusionen. Es wird sicher
sehr schwer sein. Aber ich

218

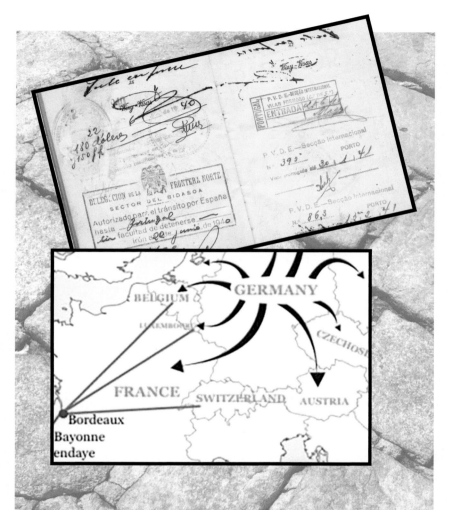

PART 4
DOCUMENTS, VISAS,
ARTIFACTS

Drawings created
by Henni, age 11,
at Hebrew school
(found by
Hilde Jakobs).

221

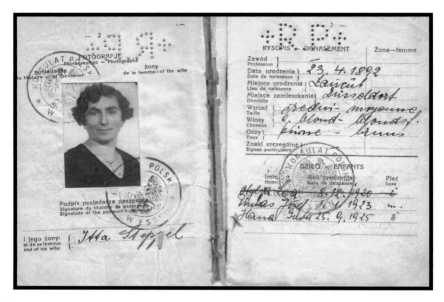

Itta Steppel's Polish passport, which confirms her birthday
as 1892, four years older than my grandfather, Moses.

A very telling page from Leah's visa: On the left side it
is stamped "permission to transport through Spain *hasta*
(until) Portugal – June 22, 1940." On the right we see the
stamp *entrada*, (enter) for Vilar Formoso.

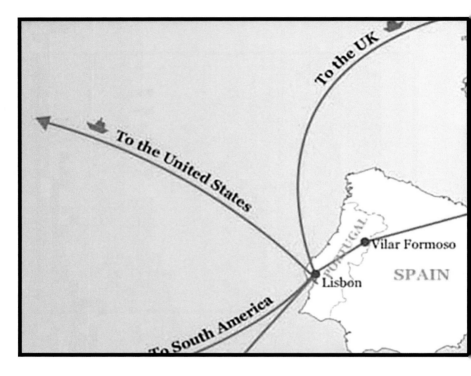

Our journey from Bordeaux, France to Lisbon,
Portugal, represented only one third of the Steppels' journey,
which began in Düsseldorf, Germany. Viewing the map on this
and the following page, compare the many
refugees' paths to the guide Leah provides us.

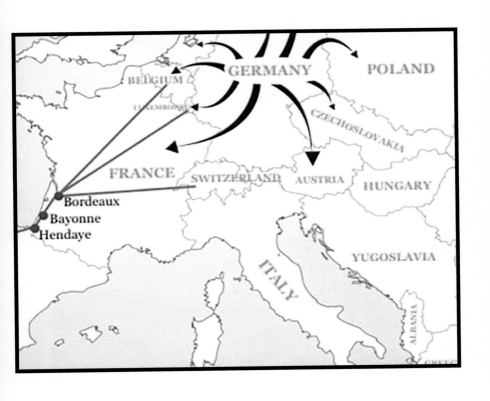

225

Düsseldorf 1938 phone directory with the Steppel name

246   Kasernenstraß

51 (E Düsseldorfer Tageblatt, Bastionstraße 14)
Wiedemeyer, Karl, Uhr-
    macher   U
Westerhuis, Wilh., Kellner   2

53 E (wie Nr. 51)
Langerfeld, Gust., Wwe.,
    Speisehaus   U
Schmidt, Joh., Arbeiter   1
→ Steppel, Moritz, Vertreter   1
Recker, Felix, o. G.   1
Stumpf, Christian, Schmied 2
Maleite, Fried., Wwe., o. G. 2

Portugal via Espana at Hendaye. 22, June, 1940

Above: Pincus (Paul) in his Army uniform.
Below: Paul returns to Europe with the
American army.

NATIONAL JEWISH WELFARE BOARD
BUREAU OF WAR RECORDS
MASTER CARD SYSTEM

AUTHENTICATED   **WOUNDED**

NAME __STEPPEL__ __Paul__ _____ RANK __Pvt.__ _____ AGE __21__
     LAST (CAPS)   FIRST   MIDDLE

NEXT OF KIN __Mr. Morris Steppel__ _____ RELATIONSHIP __Father__

ADDRESS __1529 Minford Place__ _____ CITY __Bronx__ _____ STATE __N.Y.__

SOURCE OF INFORMATION __War Dept. Rel. 3/11/44 pg. 1033__

INQUIRY DATE __6/8/44*__ _____ FOLLOW-UP DATES _____

WORKER CONSULTED __Rubinstein*__ _____ FAMILY _____

DATE APPEARED IN HONOR ROLL _____

Above and below: After returning from the European
front, Paul was wounded and received
a Purple Heart.

AWARD
NATIONAL JEWISH WELFARE BOARD
BUREAU OF WAR RECORDS
ALPHABETICAL CARD

AUTHENTICATED

PURPLE HEART

Last Name (Caps)	First	Middle	Rank	Serial #	Age
STEPPEL	Paul		Pvt.		

Next of Kin _____ Relationship _____
__Mr. Morris Steppel__ _____ __Father__
Address _____ City __Bronx.__ State __N. Y.__ Credit

Source of Information
__IBM Correction List   6/46   sbr__
Branch of Service _____ Action Area _____ Honor Roll Date _____
__Army__
Worker Consulted _____ Family _____

Inquiry Date _____ Follow-Up Dates _____
__none__

$

Margaret and H.A. Rey and Salvador Dali were among the notables spared because they received a signed visa in Bordeaux by Aristides de Sousa Mendes.

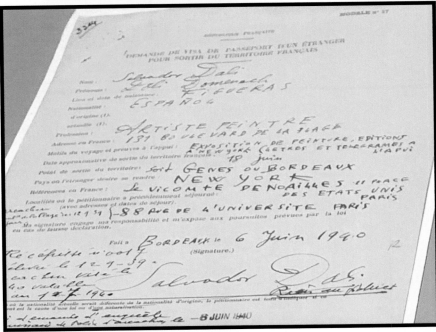

Itta's visa stamped in Bordeaux allowing her to travel
through Spain to Vilar Formoso, Portugal. We can
assume Henni and Paul were with her,
as well as Moses and Leah.

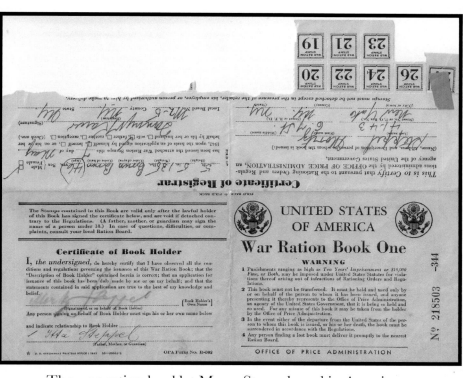

The war ration booklet Moses Steppel used in America.

Steppel cousins reunion at the
Sousa Mendes Gala, Road to Freedom.

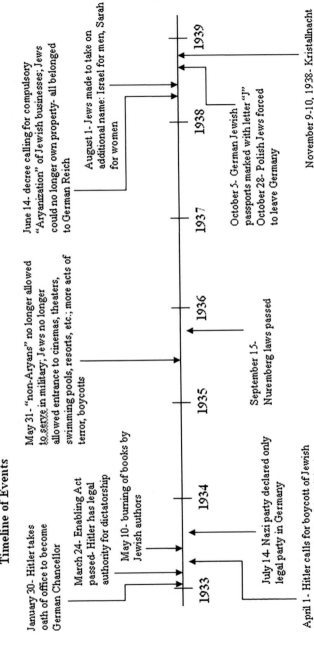

Timeline of Events

World events leading up to the Steppels' escape.

Discussion Topics

1. What attributes do you believe a person, such as Leah Steppel, caused her to painstakingly write and recount events during a nearly two-year journey? How might writing in a journal impact your decision-making process?

2. Describe how you would feel if you watched your much younger brother or sister being sent away?

3. What information has not been revealed about the toddler child, Carolina? Did all the Steppel children know about her birth, and if they knew, were they told about the infant's disability? Is there a possibility siblings were told she died at birth? Why, and to what purpose?

4. When writing her diary, Leah was meticulous regarding record keeping. What does this trait tell you about her?

5. At one point leading her family during the journey, Leah took a wrong turn which resulted in her younger brother Paul's conscription into the French Foreign Legion. What emotions would you experience after such a mistake?

6. What internal and external support systems were available to Leah during different parts of her journey?

7. What attributes of Leah do you most admire and why?

(Author's note: There are many other discussion topics that may come to mind. Feel free to expand on those written above.)

YOU MAY EMAIL REBECCA
at leahsfootsteps@gmail.com.

A Mirror And A Warning

I find myself today in a turmoil unlike anything I have experienced since discovering my mother's diaries in 1982.

> *Breaking news: Shabbat, October 27, 2018, the deadliest attack on Jews occurred in Pittsburgh's Tree of Life Synagogue and sadly earned the title, "the deadliest slaughter of Jews in United States history. Gunman 'just wanted to kill Jews.'"*

This, after scores of Jewish Community Center bomb threats, college groups shouting anti-Jewish, anti-Israel rhetoric, putting our young, talented Jewish students at risk.

The anti-Semitic hate crimes that have viciously taken so many of our brothers and sisters is incomprehensible. The division between friends, torn apart because they can no longer stand the sight of one another, due to the political stance each has chosen, is maddening.

For me, it is history repeating itself, word for word. Spewing epithets of hate and venom, out-of-control men are slaughtering children and adults of all ages in sanctuaries of prayer and learning. Swastikas and stormtroopers, hate posters and guns, abound in the open. No, not 1939. This is 2018!

The words you have read from my mother's complete diary (Part 2), is her mirror and the warning. If even one reader is moved to act, vote, and stand up for humanity, then this journey I have taken will have been worth the effort and dedication.

"Recently, I am spending much time amongst us Jews. Formerly I thought we Jews are a small, wretched people, and there was reason to hate us. Today, I must change my mind: we are a good-hearted group. We rightfully call ourselves 'the chosen people.' What I now see is willingness to sacrifice and help each other unselfishly."

What has been widely circulated is the support the Pittsburgh Squirrel Hill Jewish community is receiving from within and throughout the world.

Leah's words resound. We ARE a good people.